A Taste of the Country

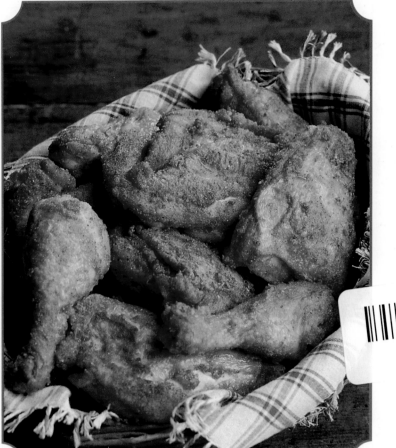

Editor: Linda Piepenbrink
Food Editor: Mary Beth Jung
Assistant Editor: Kristine Krueger
Art Director: Jennifer Hardison-Petty
Cover Design and Illustrations: Jim Sibilski
Production: Ellen Lloyd, Julie Wagner
Food Photography: Mike Huibregtse; Gilo Photography (front cover, pp. 8, 35, 38, 51, 68); Grace Sheldon (pp. 7, 22, 43)
Directors of Food Photography: Jim Sibilski, Peter Loomans, Judy Larson, Peggy Bjorkman, Sue Myers

©1992, Reiman Publications, L.P.
5400 S. 60th St., Greendale WI 53129
International Standard Book Number: 0-89821-098-4
Library of Congress Catalog Card Number: 92-60968

Recipes for the dishes featured on cover, back cover and above can be found on pages 75-77.

Stir up some mealtime excitement with these savory skillet dinners and stir-frys!

The eight enticing entrees shown here offer a delectable variety of good eating—beef and pork are only the beginning. From Skillet Pizza and Picadillo in Pita Bread to Sweet and Sour Pork, every recipe goes from start to finish in one dish!

SKILLETS SUPREME. Clockwise from lower left: **Skillet Pizza** (p. 11), **Fantastic Beef Fajitas** (p.11), **Meaty Spanish Rice** (p. 11), **Picadillo in Pita Bread** (p. 11), **German Pizza** (p. 12), **Spicy Beef with Peppers** (p. 12), **Bacon Jardin** (p. 12), **Sweet and Sour Pork** (p. 11).

For everyday family fare, sizzling skillet meals make super-satisfying suppers. They're also easy enough to prepare and serve on short notice when company's coming.

Take your pick of these convenient one-skillet main dishes—each one is destined to become a fast—and regular—favorite!

SENSATIONAL SUPPERS! Top to bottom: **Fruited Chops** (p. 12), **Chicken Mushroom Stir-Fry** (p. 13), **Steak Lo Mein** (p. 13), **Chili Skillet** (p. 12).

MEAL IN MINUTES

A menu you can make in 30 minutes or less!

Pastors don't work "regular" hours. So pastors' wives—like Judy King of Johnstown, Pennsylvania—can't always count on regular meal-times.

When committee meetings or visits to parishioners keep her husband past suppertime, Judy relies on recipes like the ones featured here for satisfying, speedy meals. She also finds "Meals in Minutes" menus handy when she's called on to feed neighbors or friends who occasionally need a helping hand.

"I'm basically a scratch cook," Judy says. "But making fast and easy meals during the week seems to fit our schedules better. On weekends and for special occasions, I like to take my time and prepare big meals."

Whatever she prepares, Judy credits her mom as her original inspiration in the kitchen.

"I developed my Pronto Chili recipe through trial and error," she admits. "Using tomato paste was born out of necessity when I ran out of canned tomato sauce one day!"

Judy recommends corn bread as a satisfying accompaniment to her chili. "Originally, I baked it in muffin tins —but, to save time, I switched to a baking pan." A speedy banana cream dessert makes a cool, refreshing finish after the spicy main course.

Next time the clock's ticking too fast in your kitchen, try Judy's quick, hearty chili supper—it'll warm body and soul!

PRONTO CHILI

- 1 pound ground beef
- 1 small onion, chopped
- 1 can (6 ounces) tomato paste plus 2 cans water
- 2 teaspoons chili powder
- 1 teaspoon salt
- 1/2 teaspoon cumin, optional
- 1/4 teaspoon black pepper
- 1 to 2 tablespoons brown sugar
- 1 can (16 ounces) kidney beans, rinsed and drained

Shredded cheddar cheese

In a saucepan, brown beef and onion. Drain fat. Stir in all remaining ingredients *except* cheese; cover and simmer 20 minutes. Top each serving with cheese, if desired. **Yield:** 4 servings.

CORN BREAD

- 1-1/2 cups all-purpose flour
- 3/4 cup cornmeal
- 2 tablespoons sugar
- 2 teaspoons baking powder
- 1/4 teaspoon salt
- 1 cup milk
- 1 egg, beaten
- 4 tablespoons butter *or* margarine, melted

Combine the first five ingredients. Add milk, egg and butter; stir until dry ingredients are moistened. Pour batter into a greased 8-in. x 8-in. baking pan. Bake at 400° for 20-25 minutes or until golden brown and a wooden pick inserted in center of bread comes out clean. Serve warm. **Yield:** 9 servings.

BANANA CREAM PARFAIT

- 1 package (3-1/2 ounces) instant banana pudding
- 2 cups cold milk
- 1/2 cup graham cracker crumbs
- 2 medium ripe bananas, sliced

Whipped cream
- 4 maraschino cherries, optional

Prepare pudding according to package directions, using the 2 cups cold milk. Sprinkle 1 tablespoon graham cracker crumbs into each of four parfait or dessert glasses. Top crumbs with 1/4 cup prepared pudding and *half* of the banana slices. Repeat layers of crumbs, pudding and banana slices. Top each dessert with a dollop of whipped cream and garnish with a cherry, if desired. **Yield:** 4 servings.

7

Next time you're hungry for the taste of a cozy, home-cooked meal, pull up your chair to a hearty meatball-and-vegetable stew with thick slices of hot homemade bread. For a satisfying finish, try whole wheat gingerbread squares topped with chilled whipped cream. Now that's a wholesome country meal!

COMFORT FOOD: Meatball Garden Stew (p. 13), No-Knead Honey Oatmeal Bread (p. 13), **Whole Wheat Gingerbread** (p. 14).

BEST COOK

Donna Patterson
Davenport, Iowa

Donna Patterson of Davenport, Iowa does all her cooking on a grand scale, whether she's working as head baker at an area hospital or treating dozens of friends to a barbecue!

"During the week, Donna cooks for the patients and hospital cafeteria at Franciscan Hospital in Rock Island, Illinois," says Kay Moneysmith, who nominated her friend. "And when we hold our yearly harvest dinner at church for some 300 people, you'll find Donna cooking there, too!"

But Donna doesn't stop there.

"She and her husband, Wayne, annually host an outdoor party for 75 to 100 friends from church to celebrate their wedding anniversary," Kay says. "Donna prepares *all* the food, and it's a real feast—barbecued ribs, fried chicken, at least a dozen different salads, pies, cakes, cookies…you name it, she serves it!"

According to Donna, "The barbecue is our way of showing friends how much we love and appreciate them. It started out very simply, but as our circle of friends grew, so did the size of our barbecue!"

Donna learned how to cook as a teenager. "My mother turned over all the household cooking chores to me for one summer," she says with a grin.

"It was sink or swim. Believe me, I learned a lot, although my father and brother suffered for a while!"

Her first dishes were simple—meat, potatoes, and vegetables from the garden. That was acceptable for the hardworking family.

"After I left home, my interests began to widen," she says. "I learned how to make some more unusual dishes, and I grew to love baking and making salads. For a while I worked in the bakery department at Drake University in Des Moines, baking for about 1,700 students. That gave me *lots* of new ideas!"

Help yourself to Donna's Lasagna (shown at left) and to a couple more of her delicious recipes.

DONNA'S LASAGNA

1 pound lean ground beef
8 ounces mild *or* hot Italian sausage
1 can (14-1/2 ounces) tomatoes, pureed
2 cans (6 ounces *each)* tomato paste
2 tablespoons sugar
3 tablespoons dried parsley, *divided*
1 tablespoon dried basil
1 garlic clove, minced
1-1/2 teaspoons salt, *divided*
9 lasagna noodles (about 8 ounces)
3 cups (24 ounces) cream-style cottage cheese
2 eggs, beaten
1/2 teaspoon pepper
1/2 cup grated Parmesan cheese
16 ounces mozzarella cheese, thinly sliced

In a Dutch oven, brown ground beef and sausage; drain excess fat. Add pureed tomatoes, tomato paste, sugar, 1 tablespoon parsley, basil, garlic and 1 teaspoon salt; simmer, uncovered, 30 minutes. Meanwhile, cook lasagna noodles in boiling water. Drain; rinse in cold water. In a bowl, combine cottage cheese, eggs, pepper, Parmesan cheese, and remaining parsley and salt. In a 13-in. x 9-in. x 2-in. pan, layer one-third of noodles, one-third of the cheese mixture, one-third of mozzarella cheese and one-third of meat sauce. Repeat layers twice. Bake at 350° for 1 hour or until heated through. Let stand 15 minutes before cutting. **Yield:** 12 servings.

PORK ORIENTAL

1 tablespoon cooking oil
1-1/2 pounds lean boneless pork, cut into bite-size pieces
1/4 cup water
1/4 cup packed brown sugar
2 tablespoons cornstarch
1 can (20 ounces) pineapple chunks, juice drained and reserved
1/4 cup vinegar
1 tablespoon soy sauce
1/2 teaspoon salt
3/4 cup green pepper strips
1/4 cup thinly sliced onion
Chow mein noodles *or* cooked rice

In a skillet, heat oil on medium-high. Brown pork slowly. Add water; cover and simmer until pork is tender, about 1 hour (add more water if necessary). Meanwhile, in a large saucepan, combine brown sugar and cornstarch. Add pineapple juice, vinegar, soy sauce and salt. Cook over low heat, stirring constantly, until thick. Drain pork; add to saucepan along with pineapple, green pepper and onions. Cook for 4-5 minutes or until vegetables are crisp-tender. Serve over chow mein noodles or rice. **Yield:** 6 servings.

PEANUT BUTTER PIE

2/3 cup sugar
2-1/2 tablespoons cornstarch
1 tablespoon all-purpose flour
1/2 teaspoon salt
3 cups milk
3 egg yolks, beaten
1/2 cup creamy peanut butter
1 pastry shell (9 inches), baked
Whipped cream *or* topping

In a saucepan, stir together sugar, cornstarch, flour and salt. Gradually add milk. Cook and stir over medium-high heat until thickened and bubbly. Reduce heat; cook and stir 2 minutes longer. Remove from the heat. Stir about 1 cup of mixture into egg yolks; return all to saucepan. Return to heat and bring to a gentle boil, stirring constantly. Cook and stir 2 minutes more. Remove from heat; stir in peanut butter until smooth. Pour into the pastry shell; cool. Cover and store in the refrigerator. Serve with whipped cream or topping. **Yield:** 8 servings.

'My Most Memorable Meal'

I consider New Mexico my home—I've lived here since 1956—but I have plenty of wonderful, warm memories of my growing-up years in the Midwest," says Norma Erne of Albuquerque.

"I can still recall those long, cold winters in Illinois. In those days, we didn't have school buses. One of your parents drove you to school or you walked."

Norma grew up in Peoria and had to trudge a long way through snow on bitter cold days. "I can still remember coming home from school to a cozy, warm kitchen, and Mom would have a pot of chili cooking. It smelled *so good*."

Although chili is considerably different in the Southwest, Norma says the chili her mother made has always been her favorite. "Just talking about it makes me want to cook up a pot!" Norma smiles. "It and the foods that Mom served with it are easily *my most memorable meal*."

"In addition to the chili, corn bread was regularly served as part of the meal—the two just go hand in hand," she confirms. "And the devil's food cake was a fitting finale after we warmed up with the chili."

As for the cocoa, Norma says her mother created a recipe that, ironically, is customary in the Southwest. "Down here, cocoa is always made with cinnamon," she explains. "Mom never knew that, of course, but she always made her cocoa with cinnamon sticks."

Every now and then, Norma gets hungry for her memorable meal of Peoria chili, corn bread, cake and cocoa. Then she's off to the kitchen...cooking up a piece of her past!

CHERISHED CHILI. Clockwise from bottom: **Peoria Chili, Hot Cinnamon Cocoa, Mom's Corn Bread, Devil's Food Cake.** All recipes on page 14.

SKILLET PIZZA

Darlene Markel, Roseburg, Oregon

(PICTURED ON PAGE 4)

1 package (6-1/2 ounces) pizza
  crust mix
1 can (8 ounces) tomato sauce
1 teaspoon Italian seasoning
1/2 teaspoon oregano
1/2 cup pepperoni slices
1/4 cup chopped onion
1/4 cup chopped green pepper
1/4 cup sliced black olives
2 cups (8 ounces) shredded
  mozzarella cheese

Grease a 12-in. electric or stove-top skillet. Prepare pizza crust according to package directions. Line bottom and 1/2 in. up the sides of the skillet with dough. Combine tomato sauce, Italian seasoning and oregano; spread over dough. Layer pepperoni, onion, green pepper and olives over sauce; sprinkle with cheese. Cover and cook over medium heat (set electric skillet to 375°) for 15 minutes or until crust is brown on bottom and cheese is melted. Slide out onto a cutting board and cut into wedges or squares. Serve immediately. **Yield:** 1 pizza (12 inches).

FANTASTIC BEEF FAJITAS

Marla Brenneman, Goshen, Indiana

(PICTURED ON PAGE 4)

1 pound sirloin *or* flank steak,
  trimmed and cut across the
  grain into 1/4-inch strips
MARINADE:
3 tablespoons cooking oil
2 tablespoons lemon juice
1 teaspoon dried oregano
1 garlic clove, minced
1/4 teaspoon salt
1/4 teaspoon pepper
FAJITAS:
2 tablespoons cooking oil,
  divided
1/2 medium onion, sliced
1 medium sweet red pepper,
  sliced into thin strips
8 flour tortillas, warmed
2 avocados, peeled and sliced
Salsa
Sour cream

In a small bowl, combine all marinade ingredients; toss with beef. Cover and refrigerate 3-6 hours or overnight, stirring several times. Drain meat before cooking. In a skillet, heat 1 tablespoon oil. Saute onion and pepper until crisp-tender; remove from pan. Add remain-

ing oil and saute meat until no longer pink, about 4 minutes. Add vegetables to pan and heat through. To serve, place a spoonful of meat/vegetable mixture on a warmed tortilla and top with avocado, salsa and sour cream. Roll tortilla around filling. **Yield:** 4-6 servings.

MEATY SPANISH RICE

Margaret Shauers, Great Bend, Kansas

(PICTURED ON PAGE 4)

 This tasty dish uses less sugar, salt and fat. Recipe includes *Diabetic Exchanges.*

2 tablespoons butter *or*
  margarine
1/2 pound ground turkey
1 medium onion, chopped
1 medium green pepper,
  chopped
2 cups water
1 can (8 ounces) tomato sauce
1 cup uncooked long-grain rice
2 tablespoons Worcestershire
  sauce
1/2 teaspoon chili powder
1/2 teaspoon dried thyme
1/4 teaspoon hot pepper sauce
1/8 teaspoon cayenne pepper,
  optional
Black pepper to taste

In a skillet, melt butter over medium heat. Add the ground turkey, onion and green pepper; cook until meat is brown and vegetables are tender. Add all of remaining ingredients and bring to a boil. Reduce heat; cover and simmer until rice is tender, about 30 minutes. **Yield:** 4 servings. **Diabetic Exchanges:** One serving (using margarine) equals 2 meat, 1-3/4 starch, 1 fat; also, 300 calories, 379 mg sodium, 52 mg cholesterol, 27 gm carbohydrate, 17 gm protein, 14 gm fat.

SWEET AND SOUR PORK

Sally Pelszynski, Princeton, Illinois

(PICTURED ON PAGE 4)

1 tablespoon cooking oil
1 pound pork loin, cut into
  1-inch cubes
1 teaspoon paprika
1/3 cup water
3 tablespoons brown sugar
2 tablespoons cornstarch
1/2 teaspoon salt
1 can (20 ounces) pineapple
  chunks, juice drained and
  reserved
1/3 cup vinegar

1 tablespoon soy sauce
1 teaspoon Worcestershire
  sauce
1 green pepper, sliced
1 small onion, sliced
1 can (8 ounces) sliced water
  chestnuts, drained
Cooked rice

In a wok or skillet, heat oil over medium-high. Add pork; sprinkle with paprika. Brown pork on all sides. Reduce heat. Add water; cover and simmer until meat is tender, about 20-25 minutes. Meanwhile, in a medium bowl, combine brown sugar, cornstarch and salt. Gradually add reserved pineapple juice, vinegar, soy sauce and Worcestershire sauce; blend until smooth. Increase temperature to medium. Stir cornstarch mixture into pork; cook, stirring constantly, until thick and bubbly. Cook and stir 2 minutes more. Stir in pineapple, green pepper, onion and water chestnuts; cover and simmer 5 minutes more or until vegetables are crisp-tender. Serve immediately over hot cooked rice. **Yield:** 4-6 servings.

PICADILLO IN PITA BREAD

Shirley Smith, Orange, California

(PICTURED ON PAGE 5)

1 pound ground beef
1 garlic clove, minced
1/2 medium onion, chopped
1 small apple, peeled, cored
  and chopped
1/4 cup beef broth
1 tablespoon vinegar
1 can (8 ounces) tomato sauce
  or 1 can (7-3/4 ounces)
  Mexican-style hot tomato
  sauce
1 teaspoon salt
1/2 teaspoon ground cinnamon
1/2 teaspoon ground cumin
1/4 cup raisins
1/3 cup sliced almonds
3 pita breads, halved
1 avocado, sliced
1/2 cup sour cream

In a large skillet over medium heat, cook beef, garlic and onion until beef is brown and onion is soft. Drain fat. Stir in apple, broth, vinegar, tomato sauce, salt, cinnamon and cumin; simmer, stirring occasionally, until the liquid is absorbed, about 15 minutes. Stir in raisins and almonds. Adjust seasoning if necessary. To serve, fill each pita half with beef mixture and top with an avocado slice and a dollop of sour cream. **Yield:** 6 servings.

GERMAN PIZZA
Audrey Nolt, Versailles, Missouri

(PICTURED ON PAGE 5)

1 pound ground beef
1/2 medium onion, chopped
1/2 green pepper, diced
1-1/2 teaspoons salt, *divided*
1/2 teaspoon pepper
2 tablespoons butter *or*
margarine
6 medium potatoes (about 2-1/4
pounds), peeled and finely
shredded
3 eggs, beaten
1/3 cup milk
2 cups (8 ounces) shredded
cheddar *or* **mozzarella cheese**

In a 12-in. stove-top or electric skillet over medium heat, brown beef with onion, green pepper, 1/2 teaspoon salt and pepper. Remove meat mixture from skillet and drain fat. Reduce heat to low. Melt butter; spread potatoes over butter and sprinkle with remaining salt. Top with beef mixture. Combine eggs and milk; pour over all. Cook, covered, until potatoes are tender, about 30 minutes. Top with cheese; cover and heat until cheese is melted, about 5 minutes. Cut into wedges or squares to serve. **Yield:** 4-6 servings.

SPICY BEEF WITH PEPPERS
Patricia Ann Fredell, Orion, Illinois

(PICTURED ON PAGE 5)

2 tablespoons cornstarch,
divided
4 tablespoons dry sherry *or*
beef broth, *divided*
4 tablespoons soy sauce,
divided
1 garlic clove, minced
1/2 to 1 teaspoon crushed dried
red pepper
1 pound top sirloin, thinly
sliced diagonally
1/2 cup water
3 tablespoons cooking oil,
divided
1 green pepper, seeded and cut
into strips
1 sweet red pepper, seeded and
cut into strips
Cooked rice *or* **chow mein noodles**

In a medium bowl, combine 1 tablespoon of the cornstarch with 2 tablespoons of sherry or broth, 2 tablespoons soy sauce, garlic and dried red pepper. Add beef and toss to coat. Set aside. In a small bowl, combine water

with remaining cornstarch, sherry and soy sauce. Set aside. In a wok or skillet, heat 1 tablespoon oil on medium-high. Add green and red peppers; stir-fry 1 minute. Remove peppers to a platter. Add remaining oil and *half* the beef; stir-fry until beef is no longer pink. Remove and stir-fry remaining beef. Return peppers and beef to pan. Stir cornstarch mixture and add to pan; bring to a boil, stirring constantly. Cook 1 minute. Serve immediately with rice or chow mein noodles. **Yield:** 4-6 servings.

BACON JARDIN
Sue Dragon, Orlando, Florida

(PICTURED ON PAGE 5)

1/2 pound sliced bacon, cut into
1-inch pieces
3/4 cup instant rice, uncooked
3/4 cup boiling water
1 small zucchini, sliced
1/4 teaspoon oregano
1 tomato, sliced
1 small onion, sliced
1 small green pepper, sliced
Pepper to taste
4 slices American cheese

In a skillet over medium-high heat, fry bacon until crisp. Pour off fat. Add rice, water and zucchini; sprinkle with the oregano. Arrange tomato, onion and green pepper over the bacon mixture; sprinkle with pepper. Cover and simmer for 10 minutes or until vegetables are crisp-tender. Top with cheese and heat only until melted. **Yield:** 4 servings.

FRUITED CHOPS
Teresa Lillycrop, Puslinch, Ontario

(PICTURED ON PAGE 6)

1 tablespoon cooking oil
4 pork chops, about 1 inch
thick
1 can (10-3/4 ounces)
condensed chicken broth
2 tablespoons soy sauce
1 tablespoon vinegar
1/2 cup apple juice
2 tablespoons brown sugar
2 tablespoons cornstarch
1 teaspoon ground ginger
1 large apple, cored and
coarsely chopped
Cooked rice
Sliced green onions

In a 10-in. skillet, heat oil over medium-high. Brown chops on both sides.

Stir in chicken broth, soy sauce and vinegar; bring to a boil. Reduce heat, cover and simmer 20 minutes or until chops are tender. Meanwhile, in a small bowl, combine apple juice, brown sugar, cornstarch and ginger; stir until smooth. Remove chops from skillet and keep warm. Increase heat to medium. Stir cornstarch mixture into skillet; cook and stir until thickened. Add chopped apple and heat through. On a platter, arrange chops over rice. Spoon sauce over chops and top with green onions. **Yield:** 4 servings.

CHILI SKILLET
Katherine Brown, Fredericktown, Ohio

(PICTURED ON PAGE 6)

1 pound ground beef
1 cup chopped onion
1/2 cup chopped green pepper
1 garlic clove, minced
1 cup tomato juice
1 can (8 ounces) red kidney
beans, undrained
4 teaspoons chili powder
1 teaspoon dried oregano
1 teaspoon salt
1/2 cup uncooked long-grain rice
1 cup canned *or* **frozen corn**
1/2 cup sliced black olives
1 cup (4 ounces) shredded
cheddar *or* **Monterey Jack**
cheese

In a large skillet over medium heat, cook beef, onion, pepper and garlic until meat is brown and vegetables are tender. Drain fat. Add the tomato juice, kidney beans, chili powder, oregano, salt and rice; cover and simmer about 25 minutes or until rice is tender. Stir in corn and olives; cover and cook 5 minutes more. Sprinkle with cheese, cover and cook only until cheese melts, about 5 minutes. **Yield:** 4 servings.

SAVVY STIR-FRYING: To prevent uneven cooking when stir-frying in a wok or large skillet, keep the foods in constant motion.

❖Make additional sauce in a separate pan to serve at the table. It's great over rice!

❖When using leftover cooked chicken (or any other cooked meat) in stir-fry recipes, add it last and cook just long enough to heat.

❖If fresh gingerroot is available only occasionally in your area, mince it and freeze in measured portions to fit your recipes. Wrap well to avoid freezer burn.

STEAK LO MEIN

Jo Groth, Plainfield, Iowa

(PICTURED ON PAGE 6)

 This tasty dish uses less sugar, salt and fat. Recipe includes *Diabetic Exchanges*.

- 1 pound round steak, trimmed
- 1 teaspoon beef bouillon granules
- 3/4 cup water
- 1/4 cup soy sauce
- 2 tablespoons cornstarch
- 2 tablespoons cooking oil
- 1 garlic clove, minced
- 2 cups shredded cabbage
- 1 cup diagonally sliced carrots, partially cooked
- 1 medium onion, sliced into rings
- 1/2 cup sliced fresh mushrooms
- 1/2 cup diagonally sliced celery
- 1/3 cup sliced green onions
- 15 fresh snow pea pods, trimmed
- 1 can (8 ounces) sliced water chestnuts, drained
- 4 ounces thin spaghetti, cooked and drained

Freeze steak just until firm; slice diagonally across grain into 1/4-in. strips. Combine bouillon, water, soy sauce and cornstarch. Set aside. In a wok or large skillet, heat oil on medium-high. Add meat and garlic; stir-fry until the meat is no longer pink, about 5 minutes. Remove meat to a platter. Add cabbage, carrots, onion, mushrooms, celery and green onions; stir-fry for about 3 minutes. Add pea pods and water chestnuts; stir-fry 2 minutes. Add meat. Stir bouillon mixture and pour into skillet; cook and stir until thickened. Gently toss in spaghetti and heat through for 1 minute. **Yield:** 6 servings. **Diabetic Exchanges:** One serving equals 2 lean meat, 1-3/4 starch, 1 vegetable; also, 329 calories, 834 mg sodium, 52 mg cholesterol, 34 gm carbohydrate, 29 gm protein, 8 gm fat.

CHICKEN MUSHROOM STIR-FRY

Christina Thompson, Howell, Michigan

(PICTURED ON PAGE 6)

 This tasty dish uses less sugar, salt and fat. Recipe includes *Diabetic Exchanges*.

- 1 tablespoon soy sauce
- 1 egg white
- 1 teaspoon sesame oil
- 1/2 teaspoon brown sugar
- 1 teaspoon cornstarch
- 1/8 teaspoon white pepper
- 1 pound boneless chicken breasts, cut into 1/2-inch cubes
- 1/2 cup chicken broth
- 2 tablespoons cornstarch
- 2 tablespoons cold water
- 1/4 cup oyster sauce
- 4 tablespoons cooking oil, *divided*
- 1-1/2 teaspoons minced fresh gingerroot
- 2 garlic cloves, minced
- 2 green onions, sliced
- 4 medium carrots, cubed
- 1 pound fresh mushrooms, quartered
- 1/4 pound fresh snow pea pods, trimmed and cut in half

Combine first six ingredients; toss with chicken. Refrigerate 30 minutes. In a small bowl, combine chicken broth, cornstarch, water and oyster sauce. Set aside. In a wok or large skillet, heat 2 tablespoons oil over medium-high. Add gingerroot, garlic and onions; stir-fry 1 minute. Add chicken and continue to stir-fry until the chicken is white. Remove chicken and vegetables from pan. Add remaining oil; stir-fry carrots 3 minutes or until crisp-tender. Add mushrooms and pea pods; stir-fry 1 minute. Return chicken and vegetables to pan. Stir broth mixture and pour into skillet; cook and stir until the sauce is thickened. Serve immediately. **Yield:** 6 servings. **Diabetic Exchanges:** One serving equals 3 lean meat, 3/4 starch, 1 vegetable, 1 fat; also, 299 calories, 431 mg sodium, 68 mg cholesterol, 15 gm carbohydrate, 30 gm protein, 14 gm fat.

MEATBALL GARDEN STEW

Bev Hurst, Sweet Home, Oregon

(PICTURED ON PAGE 8)

- 1 pound lean ground beef
- 4 tablespoons all-purpose flour, *divided*
- 1 teaspoon salt

Dash pepper

- 1 egg
- 1/4 cup milk
- 1/4 cup chopped onion
- 1 tablespoon butter *or* margarine
- 1 garlic clove, minced
- 1 can (14-1/2 ounces) beef broth
- 2/3 cup water
- 1/2 teaspoon dried thyme
- 6 medium potatoes, peeled and quartered
- 6 medium carrots, halved lengthwise and crosswise
- 6 green onions, chopped
- 1 package (10 ounces) frozen peas, defrosted

In a medium bowl, combine beef, 2 tablespoons flour, salt, pepper, egg, milk and onion. Form into 1-in. balls. Melt butter in a large skillet or Dutch oven. Saute garlic for 1 minute. Brown meatballs on all sides. Push the meatballs to the side. Blend remaining flour into the drippings. Add the broth, water and thyme. Cook, stirring constantly, until thickened. Add potatoes, carrots and onions and stir with meatballs and sauce. Cover and simmer until vegetables are tender, about 30-35 minutes. Add peas and continue to cook 10 minutes. Adjust seasonings, if desired. **Yield:** 6 servings.

NO-KNEAD HONEY OATMEAL BREAD

Janice Dancer, Williamstown, Vermont

(PICTURED ON PAGE 8)

 This tasty dish uses less sugar, salt and fat. Recipe includes *Diabetic Exchanges*.

- 2 cups water, *divided*
- 1 cup rolled oats
- 1/3 cup butter *or* margarine, softened
- 1/3 cup honey
- 1 tablespoon salt
- 2 packages (1/4 ounce *each*) active dry yeast
- 1 egg
- 4 to 5 cups all-purpose flour, *divided*

Melted butter *or* margarine

In a saucepan, heat 1 cup water to boiling. Stir in oats, butter, honey and salt. Cool to lukewarm. Heat remaining water to 110°-115° and dissolve yeast. In a large mixing bowl, combine yeast mixture, egg, 2 cups flour and the oats mixture. Beat until the ingredients are combined and the batter is smooth. By hand, add enough remaining flour to make a stiff batter. Spread batter evenly into two greased 8-1/2-in. x 4-1/2-in. x 2-1/2-in. loaf pans. Smooth tops of loaves. Cover and let rise in a warm place until doubled, about 35-40 minutes. Bake at 375° for 40-45 minutes. Remove from pans and brush with melted butter, if desired. **Yield:** 2 loaves. **Diabetic Exchanges:** One slice equals 1 starch; also, 81 calories, 175 mg sodium, 6 mg cholesterol, 14 gm carbohydrate, 2 gm protein, 2 gm fat.

MEMORABLE MEAL

The following four recipes come from Norma Erne of Albuquerque, New Mexico (see photo and story on page 10).

PEORIA CHILI

 This tasty dish uses less sugar, salt and fat. Recipe includes *Diabetic Exchanges.*

2 pounds ground beef
1 medium onion, chopped
1 can (28 ounces) whole tomatoes with liquid, chopped
1 can (46 ounces) tomato juice
1 to 2 tablespoons chili powder
1 tablespoon sugar
Salt and pepper to taste
2 cans (15 ounces *each*) red kidney beans, rinsed and drained
Shredded cheddar cheese, optional

In a large kettle or Dutch oven, brown beef and onion. Drain off fat; add all remaining ingredients except beans and cheese. Cover and simmer 2-3 hours. Adjust seasonings, if necessary. Stir in beans and heat through. Before serving, top with shredded cheddar cheese, if desired. **Yield:** 10 servings. **Diabetic Exchanges:** One serving equals 3 lean meat, 1-1/2 starch, 1 vegetable; also, 288 calories, 826 mg sodium, 64 mg cholesterol, 28 gm carbohydrate, 26 gm protein, 9 gm fat. **If Cooking For Two:** Freeze chili in serving-size portions for quick meals later.

MOM'S CORN BREAD

2 eggs, beaten
1-1/4 cups milk
1/4 cup shortening *or* bacon fat, melted
1-1/2 cups yellow cornmeal
3/4 cup all-purpose flour
2 tablespoons sugar
2-1/4 teaspoons baking powder
1 teaspoon salt

Combine eggs, milk and shortening. Sift together all remaining ingredients and add to egg mixture; stir only until blended. Pour into a greased 8-in. x 8-in. baking pan. Bake at 400° for 20-25 minutes, or until bread shrinks slightly from sides of the pan and begins to brown on the edges. **Yield:** about 9 servings.

HOT CINNAMON COCOA

1/4 cup baking cocoa
1/4 cup sugar
1/8 teaspoon salt
1 cup boiling water
3 cups scalded milk
2 cinnamon sticks (about 3 inches *each*)
1 teaspoon vanilla extract

In the top of a double boiler, stir together cocoa, sugar and salt. Gradually add boiling water. Place over direct heat and boil for 2 minutes, stirring constantly. Add milk and cinnamon sticks and place over boiling water. Stir and heat 10 minutes. Remove sticks and stir in vanilla. Beat with a wire whisk to froth milk. Serve immediately. **Yield:** about 4 servings.

DUST WITH COCOA: When baking a chocolate cake, dust your greased baking pans with unsweetened cocoa instead of flour to avoid that white "floury" look.

DEVIL'S FOOD CAKE

2 cups packed brown sugar
1/2 cup shortening
2 eggs
1 teaspoon vanilla extract
2-1/2 cups all-purpose flour
1/3 cup baking cocoa
1 teaspoon baking powder
1/2 teaspoon baking soda
1/4 teaspoon salt
1 cup sour milk* *or* whey
FROSTING:
2 egg whites
1-1/2 cups sugar
5 tablespoons water
1-1/2 teaspoons light corn syrup
1 teaspoon vanilla extract

In a large mixing bowl, combine brown sugar, shortening and eggs. Add vanilla; beat well. Sift together flour, cocoa, baking powder, soda and salt. Add alternately with milk or whey to the egg mixture. Pour batter into 2 greased 9-in. round cake pans. Bake at 350° for 30 minutes or until cake tests done. Cool 5 minutes before removing to a wire rack. Continue to cool. For frosting, combine first four ingredients in the top of a double boiler; beat with an electric mixer until thoroughly mixed. Place over rapidly boiling water and continue to beat for 7 minutes or until frosting will hold stiff peaks. Remove from boiling water and add vanilla. Continue to beat frosting until thick enough to spread. Frost cake when completely cooled. **Yield:** 12-14 servings. *To sour milk, place 1 tablespoon white vinegar in a measuring cup; add enough milk to equal 1 cup.

WHOLE WHEAT GINGERBREAD
Patricia Habiger, Spearville, Kansas

(PICTURED ON PAGE 8)

1 cup molasses
3/4 cup honey
3/4 cup vegetable oil
3 eggs
3 cups whole wheat flour
1 tablespoon baking powder
1 teaspoon salt
1-1/2 teaspoons ground cinnamon
1-1/2 teaspoons ground cloves
1 teaspoon ground ginger
2 cups milk
Whipped cream

In a large mixing bowl, beat molasses, honey, oil and eggs until well-mixed. Combine dry ingredients and add alternately with the milk to the egg mixture. Pour batter into a greased 13-in. x 9-in. x 2-in. baking pan. Bake at 350° for 45-50 minutes or until a toothpick inserted in the center comes out clean. Serve warm or at room temperature with chilled whipped cream. **Yield:** 12-15 servings.

CARAMEL PUDDING
Mary Ann Smucker, Lykens, Pennsylvania

6 cups milk
3 eggs
1-1/2 cups packed brown sugar
1/2 cup sugar
3/4 cup all-purpose flour
2 teaspoons vanilla extract
2 tablespoons butter *or* margarine

In a large saucepan, scald milk. Meanwhile, in a mixing bowl, beat eggs until creamy. Add sugars, flour and 1-1/2 cups of the scalded milk; slowly pour into saucepan with remaining milk. Cook and stir over medium heat until pudding thickens, about 15-20 minutes. Remove from heat; add vanilla and butter. Stir well. Continue to stir pudding every 10 minutes until cooled. **Yield:** 15 servings.

SKILLET CHICKEN AND ARTICHOKES

Jody Steinke, Nekoosa, Wisconsin

4 large boneless chicken breast
   halves
3/4 teaspoon salt-free herb
   seasoning
1 jar (6 ounces) marinated
   artichoke hearts, drained and
   marinade reserved
1 tablespoon all-purpose flour
1/2 cup water
1/4 cup dry white wine *or* water
1 teaspoon chicken bouillon
   granules
12 small fresh mushrooms, cut
   in half
1 tablespoon chopped fresh
   parsley
Cooked rice *or* noodles

Sprinkle chicken with herb seasoning. In a medium skillet, heat 3 tablespoons of the reserved marinade. Add chicken and brown 3-4 minutes per side. Drain all but 1 tablespoon of marinade in skillet. Push chicken to one side and stir in flour. Add water, wine and bouillon. Stir until mixture boils and sauce is lightly thickened. Stir in the artichokes and mushrooms. Cover and simmer on very low heat 20 minutes or until the chicken is tender. Sprinkle with parsley. Serve on a bed of rice or noodles. **Yield:** 4 servings.

SHIPWRECK STEW

Estelle Bates, Fallbrook, California

 This tasty dish uses less sugar, salt and fat. Recipe includes *Diabetic Exchanges.*

1 pound ground beef
1 cup chopped onion
3 cups peeled cubed potatoes
3 medium carrots, peeled and
   sliced
1 cup chopped celery
1/4 cup minced fresh parsley
1 package (9 ounces) frozen cut
   green beans, defrosted
1 can (15 ounces) kidney
   beans, rinsed and drained
1 can (8 ounces) tomato sauce
1/4 cup uncooked long-grain rice
1 teaspoon salt
1 teaspoon Worcestershire
   sauce
1/2 to 1 teaspoon chili powder
1/4 teaspoon ground pepper
1 cup water

In a skillet, brown beef with onion over medium heat. Drain fat. In a 3-qt. casserole, combine beef mixture with all remaining ingredients. Cover and bake at 350° for about 1 hour or until rice and potatoes are tender. **Yield:** 10 servings. **Diabetic Exchanges:** One serving equals 1-1/2 lean meat, 1-1/2 starch, 1 vegetable; also, 204 calories, 390 mg sodium, 32 mg cholesterol, 28 gm carbohydrate, 15 gm protein, 4 gm fat.

CURRIED CUCUMBERS

Debra Creed-Broeker, Rocky Mount, Missouri

1/3 cup sour cream
1/2 cup mayonnaise
1/4 to 1/2 teaspoon lemon pepper
1/4 to 1/2 teaspoon curry powder
1/4 teaspoon garlic salt
1/2 teaspoon parsley flakes
Hot pepper sauce to taste
   3 cucumbers, peeled and thinly
     sliced
1/2 medium onion, thinly sliced
Salt and pepper to taste
Fresh parsley *or* chopped chives,
   optional

In a bowl, combine first seven ingredients. Toss with cucumbers and onion slices. Chill 2-3 hours. Stir just before serving. Adjust salt and pepper to taste; garnish with parsley or chives, if desired. **Yield:** 6-8 servings.

ROARING TWENTIES SPICE CAKE

Loretta Saltsganer, Denver, Colorado

1 cup sugar
1 cup raisins
1/2 cup shortening
1 teaspoon ground cinnamon
1 teaspoon ground nutmeg
1/2 teaspoon ground cloves
Pinch salt
1-1/2 cups water
2 cups all-purpose flour
1 teaspoon baking powder
1 teaspoon baking soda
1 tablespoon water
NUTMEG SAUCE:
1 cup water
1/2 cup sugar
2 tablespoons cornstarch
1 tablespoon butter *or*
   margarine
1 tablespoon lemon juice
1/4 teaspoon nutmeg

Combine first eight ingredients in a saucepan and bring to a boil. Boil 5 minutes. Remove from heat and stir in flour, baking powder, and baking soda dissolved in the tablespoon of water. Mix well. Spread into a greased 8-in. x 8-in. baking pan. Bake at 350° for about 30 minutes or until a toothpick inserted in center of cake comes out clean. Meanwhile, combine sauce ingredients in a saucepan and cook over medium-low heat until thickened. Serve cake warm or room temperature with warm sauce. **Yield:** 9 servings.

HERBED MACARONI AND CHEESE

Nancy Raymond, Waldoboro, Maine

1 package (7 ounces) macaroni
2 tablespoons butter *or*
   margarine
2 tablespoons all-purpose flour
1/2 teaspoon Italian seasoning
1/4 teaspoon onion powder
Salt and pepper to taste
1 cup milk
1/4 cup sour cream
3/4 cup shredded cheddar
   cheese, *divided*
1/2 cup cubed Havarti *or*
   Muenster cheese
2 tablespoons grated Parmesan
   cheese
2 tablespoons Italian-style
   seasoned bread crumbs

Cook macaroni and drain well; place in a 1-1/2-qt. casserole and set aside. In a saucepan, melt butter over medium heat. Stir in the flour and seasonings; gradually add milk. Cook and stir until thickened. Remove pan from heat; add sour cream, 1/2 cup cheddar cheese and all the Havarti or Muenster. Stir until melted. Pour sauce over macaroni and mix well. Combine Parmesan cheese, bread crumbs and remaining cheddar cheese; sprinkle over casserole. Bake at 350° for 15-20 minutes. **Yield:** 6 servings.

NEVER-FAIL PECAN PIE

Beverly Materne, Reeves, Louisiana

2 eggs, well beaten
1/2 cup sugar
1 cup dark corn syrup
1 tablespoon all-purpose flour
1/4 teaspoon salt
1 teaspoon vanilla extract
1 cup pecan halves
1 unbaked pie shell (9 inches)

Combine eggs, sugar, corn syrup, flour, salt and vanilla. Stir in pecans. Pour into pie shell. Cover pastry edges with foil to prevent excess browning. Bake at 350° for 30 minutes. Remove foil and bake another 15 minutes or until golden brown. **Yield:** 6-8 servings.

GRANDMA'S PEA SOUP

Carole Talcott, Dahinda, Illinois

1/2 pound dried whole peas
1/2 pound dried split peas
1 ham bone
3 quarts water
1 large onion, chopped
1 carrot, chopped
2 celery stalks, chopped
Leaves from 6 celery stalks, chopped
1 teaspoon bouquet garni (mixed herbs)
1 tablespoon minced fresh parsley
1 bay leaf
1 teaspoon salt
1/4 teaspoon pepper
1/2 pound smoked cooked Thuringer, chopped, optional
SPAETZLE DUMPLINGS:
1 cup all-purpose flour
1 egg, beaten
1/3 cup water

Cover peas with water and soak overnight. Drain, rinse and place in a Dutch oven or soup kettle. Add ham bone, water and all remaining ingredients except Thuringer and dumplings. Cover and simmer over low heat 2 to 2-1/2 hours. Remove ham bone, skim any fat, and cut and dice remaining meat from bone. Add ham and Thuringer, if desired, to kettle. To prepare dumplings, put flour in a small bowl; make a depression in the center of the flour; add egg and water. Mix until smooth. Place a colander with 3/16-in.-diameter holes over simmering soup; pour batter into the colander and press through with a wooden spoon. Cook, uncovered, 10-15 minutes. Remove bay leaf. **Yield:** 4 quarts. **If Cooking for Two:** Prepare soup without dumplings and freeze in serving-size portions to enjoy for months to come.

ICEBOX ROLLS

Jean Fox, Welch, Minnesota

1 package (1/4 ounce) active dry yeast
2-1/2 cups water, *divided*
1/2 cup shortening
2 eggs, beaten
1-1/2 teaspoons salt
1/2 cup sugar
7-1/2 to 8 cups all-purpose flour
Melted butter

Dissolve yeast in 1/2 cup warm water (105°-110°). In a large mixing bowl, combine 1 cup boiling water and shortening. Add remaining water, eggs, salt, sugar and yeast mixture.

Stir in 1 cup of flour at a time, mixing well after each addition. Add enough flour to form a soft dough that can be kneaded. Turn dough out onto a floured surface and knead until smooth and elastic, about 6-8 minutes. Place in a greased bowl, turning once to grease the top. Cover and refrigerate overnight. When ready to bake, form dough into cloverleaf rolls and place in greased muffin tins. Cover and let rise in a warm place until doubled, about 1 hour. Bake at 375° for 15-20 minutes. Remove from oven and brush with melted butter. **Yield:** 36 rolls. **If Cooking for Two:** Freeze baked rolls in plastic storage bags to enjoy at a moment's notice.

BEEF-STUFFED SQUASH

Darlene R. Smith, Rockford, Illinois

3 small acorn squash, halved and seeded
1/2 cup water
FILLING:
1 pound lean ground beef
1 egg, beaten
1/2 cup Russian salad dressing
3/4 cup bread crumbs
1 medium onion, minced
1 tablespoon brown sugar
1 teaspoon lemon juice
3/4 teaspoon salt
GLAZE:
1/4 cup Russian salad dressing
1-1/2 teaspoons lemon juice
1-1/2 teaspoons brown sugar

Place squash, cut side down, in a roasting pan and pour water in pan. Bake at 350° for 30 minutes. Meanwhile, in a medium bowl, combine filling ingredients. Remove squash from oven. Increase oven temperature to 375°. Lightly spoon filling into each squash cavity. Combine glaze ingredients and baste meat and top of squash. Bake 40-50 minutes, basting with glaze every 15 minutes. **Yield:** 6 servings.

SKILLET LASAGNA

Lucinda C. Walker, Somerset, Pennsylvania

1-1/2 pounds lean ground beef
1 small onion, chopped
1 green pepper, chopped
1 jar (30 ounces) spaghetti sauce with mushrooms
1 teaspoon dried oregano
1 teaspoon dried basil
6 lasagna noodles, cooked and rinsed

3 cups (12 ounces) shredded mozzarella cheese
1/2 cup grated Parmesan cheese

In a Dutch oven, brown beef, onion and pepper. Drain fat, if necessary. Stir in spaghetti sauce, oregano and basil. Simmer, uncovered, 10-15 minutes. In a 10-in. skillet, spread 1/4 cup of the meat sauce. Top with 3 noodles, cutting to fit as needed. Spread half the remaining sauce and half the mozzarella and Parmesan cheeses. Top with remaining noodles, meat sauce and Parmesan. Cover and heat on medium for 3 minutes. Reduce heat to low; cook for 35 minutes. Sprinkle with remaining mozzarella and let stand 10 minutes with cover ajar. **Yield:** 6-8 servings.

UPSTATE CHOCOLATE PEANUT BUTTER PIE

Kim Scott, Byron, New York

1 graham cracker crust (9 inches), baked
1 cup sugar
6 tablespoons all-purpose flour
1/2 teaspoon salt
2 cups milk
3 egg yolks, beaten
1 teaspoon vanilla extract
2 tablespoons creamy peanut butter
1 ounce semisweet chocolate, melted
Whipped cream
Chopped peanuts

Prepare crust, then cool to room temperature. In the top of a double boiler, over hot but not boiling water, combine sugar, flour and salt. Slowly add milk and cook 10 minutes, stirring constantly. Pour a little hot milk mixture into the egg yolks. Immediately add egg yolk mixture to double boiler. Cook 4 minutes, stirring constantly. Stir in vanilla. Cool about 10 minutes. Divide mixture in half. To one half add peanut butter; stir well. To the remaining half add the melted chocolate. Allow mixtures to cool completely. Fill pie crust first with peanut butter mixture, then chocolate layer. Chill before serving. Top with whipped cream and nuts. **Yield:** 8 servings.

16

KIELBASA BEAN SOUP

Mary E. Cordes, Omaha, Nebraska

2 cups water
1 medium potato, peeled and diced
2 carrots, peeled and sliced
1 medium onion, chopped
1/3 cup chopped celery
8 ounces smoked kielbasa, thinly sliced
1 can (11-1/2 ounces) bean with bacon soup, undiluted
Chopped fresh parsley, optional

In a large saucepan, bring water and vegetables to a boil. Simmer 10 minutes or until vegetables are tender. Add kielbasa and soup. Heat through. Garnish with parsley, if desired. **Yield:** 6 servings.

WINTER FRUIT SALAD

Ceal Langer, Milwaukee, Wisconsin

1 can (20 ounces) pineapple chunks in natural juices, drained and juice reserved
1 package (3-1/8 ounces) cook 'n' serve vanilla pudding
1 quart mixed fresh fruit chunks (apples, bananas, oranges, pears)
3/4 cup chopped pecans *or* walnuts
1/3 cup flaked coconut
Whipped topping, optional

In a saucepan, combine reserved pineapple juice and pudding mix. Cook over medium heat until thickened; cool. Toss with pineapple chunks, fruit chunks, nuts and coconut. Chill until ready to serve. Garnish each serving with a dollop of the whipped topping, if desired. **Yield:** 6-8 servings.

ORANGE BEEF AND BROCCOLI STIR-FRY

Arly M. Schnabel, Ellendale, North Dakota

✓ This tasty dish uses less sugar, salt and fat. Recipe includes *Diabetic Exchanges*.

1 pound well-trimmed top sirloin, cut into thin strips
4 teaspoons soy sauce
2 teaspoons shredded fresh gingerroot *or* 1/2 teaspoon ground ginger
1 teaspoon finely grated orange peel
1 tablespoon vegetable oil
2 cups broccoli florets
1 small sweet red pepper, cut into strips
2/3 cup picante sauce
1/2 teaspoon sugar, optional
1/3 cup orange juice
1 tablespoon cornstarch
3 green onions with tops, cut diagonally into 1-inch pieces
Sliced almonds, optional
Hot steamed rice

Toss meat with soy sauce, ginger and orange peel; set aside for 10 minutes. Heat oil in a wok or large skillet on high. Stir-fry mixture just until meat is no longer pink; remove. Add broccoli, pepper, picante sauce and sugar to skillet. Cover and reduce heat to simmer. Cook until vegetables are crisp-tender, about 3 minutes. Combine orange juice and cornstarch; add to skillet along with meat and onions. Cook and stir 1 minute or until sauce is thickened. Sprinkle with almonds, if desired. Serve with rice. **Yield:** 4-6 servings. **Diabetic Exchanges:** One serving without rice equals 2 lean meat, 1 vegetable, 1/4 starch; also, 160 calories, 412 mg sodium, 52 mg cholesterol, 10 gm carbohydrate, 20 gm protein, 5 gm fat.

STIR-FRY STEPS. Slicing raw meat in thin strips for stir-frying is easier if you freeze it first for about 1 hour.
❖For even cooking, cut all vegetables into uniform sizes.

CHERRY SQUARES

Ann Fabian, Tilley, Alberta

FILLING:
2 cans (16 ounces *each*) tart red cherries
3/4 cup sugar
5 tablespoons cornstarch
1/4 teaspoon salt
1 tablespoon butter *or* margarine
1/2 teaspoon almond extract
Several drops red food coloring
BASE:
1 package (1/4 ounce) active dry yeast
2/3 cup warm milk (110°-115°)
1 cup butter *or* margarine
3-1/2 cups all-purpose flour
2 tablespoons sugar
1/2 teaspoon salt
5 egg yolks, beaten
TOPPING:
1/4 cup butter *or* margarine
1-1/2 cups confectioners' sugar
2 tablespoons half-and-half cream
1/2 teaspoon almond extract
3/4 cup chopped nuts

Drain cherries; reserve 1 cup of the juice. Set aside. In a saucepan, com-

bine sugar, cornstarch and salt. Stir in cherry juice. Cook and stir over medium-high heat until bubbly. Cook and stir 1 minute more. Remove from heat; stir in butter, extract, food coloring and cherries. Set aside to cool. Dissolve yeast in warm milk. Let stand 5 minutes. Cut butter into flour, sugar and salt. Add yeast mixture and egg yolks; mix thoroughly. If needed, add additional flour to make a soft dough. Turn dough out onto a lightly floured surface and knead 10 times. Divide dough in half. Roll half the dough into a 17-in. x 11-in. rectangle. Carefully transfer to a greased 17-1/2-in. x 11-1/2-in. x 1-in. baking pan. Spread cooled cherry filling over dough. Roll out second portion of dough to 17-in. x 11-in. rectangle. Carefully place over cherry filling. Press edges together to seal. Cover and allow to rise in a warm place until doubled, about 30 minutes. Bake at 350° about 25 minutes or until golden brown. Cool. Combine topping ingredients except nuts and spread over uncut surface. Top with nuts and cut into squares. **Yield:** 24 squares.

RANCH-STYLE BAKED LENTILS

Linda Lewis, Coeur d'Alene, Idaho

2 cups dry lentils (4 cups cooked)
2 teaspoons salt
5 cups water, *divided*
1 pound lean ground beef
1 envelope dry onion soup mix
1 cup catsup
1 teaspoon prepared mustard
1 teaspoon vinegar

Rinse the lentils. In a heavy saucepan, bring lentils, salt and 4 cups water to a boil. Cover and simmer 20 minutes or until the water is absorbed and the lentils are tender. Meanwhile, brown beef in a skillet. Drain excess fat. Stir in soup mix, catsup, mustard, vinegar and remaining water. Gently stir in lentils. Spoon into a 2-qt. casserole. Bake, covered, at 400° for 30-35 minutes. **Yield:** 4-6 servings.

COUNTRY INN

Mast Farm Inn

P.O. Box 704
Valle Crucis
North Carolina 28691

Phone: 1-704/963-5857

Directions: From Boone, take Hwy. 105 south to SR 1112, left 3 miles to inn.

Innkeepers: Francis and Sibyl Pressly

Schedule: Open May through October, the first two weekends in December, and also December 27 through February.

Accommodations and Rates: Ten farmhouse guest rooms, six with private bath; accommodations in loom house, blacksmith shop, woodworking shop have private baths; $75 to $140, includes breakfast and dinner. No smoking, pets or small children.

Honest food" and "comfortable country charm" are the words that best describe a relaxing stay at the Mast Farm Inn. Francis and Sibyl Pressly, the friendly hosts of the historic mountain farmstead near Valle Crucis, North Carolina, lend down-home hospitality to the scrumptious breakfasts and candlelight dinners served there.

Wake up to fresh fruit salad, orange juice, coffee and every guest's favorite: French toast stuffed with cheese.

For dinner, begin with a bowl of tomato bisque, then dig into tender roast pork loin with sweet potato and apple casserole. Delicious desserts like a moist pineapple creme cake will give you the urge to splurge.

So try these recipes and sample some "honest food" from the Mast Farm Inn...you'll feel wonderfully restored!

STUFFED FRENCH TOAST

2 loaves French bread
1 package (8 ounces) cream
    cheese, room temperature
1 carton (15 ounces) ricotta
    cheese
Peach *or* apricot preserves
2 cups milk
8 eggs
2 tablespoons vanilla extract
1/2 teaspoon salt
Ground nutmeg to taste

Slice French bread diagonally into 1/2- to 3/4-in. slices. Blend cheeses with a fork until smooth; spread on one side of each slice of bread, not quite to edges. Top cheese side of one slice of bread with 1 teaspoon preserves and press second slice of bread on top, cheese sides together. Cover with plastic wrap and refrigerate several hours or overnight. When ready to use, place bread in a single layer in shallow pan. Mix milk, eggs, vanilla, salt and nutmeg in blender. Blend 5 seconds on medium speed. Pour milk mixture over bread. Allow bread to soak a few minutes, then turn to coat other side. Remove; brown on both sides in a greased skillet. Serve immediately or put in 250° oven until serving time. Serve with raspberry jam or maple or other fruit syrup. **Yield:** 20-24 pieces.

ROAST PORK LOIN

1/2 pork loin, bones removed
    and reserved
Salt and pepper
2 tablespoons garlic powder
Water
1/2 cup all purpose flour

Season pork loin generously with salt, pepper and garlic powder. Place in a roasting pan; cover tightly with foil and roast at 350° for 1 hour. Remove foil; add 1 cup water to pan. Roast 1 more hour or until meat is tender. While pork roasts, trim fat off bones; place in pot with water to cover. Boil about an hour. Discard bones and fat. When pork is done, remove from pan onto a warm platter. Pour excess fat from pan, reserving 1/2 cup drippings. Add flour and stir over moderate heat until smooth. With a wire whisk, stir in broth from bones—begin with 2 cups, then add more if gravy is too thick. Stir and simmer at least 5 minutes. Adjust seasonings if necessary. Slice pork and top with hot gravy or serve gravy on the side. **Yield:** 8 servings.

SWEET POTATO AND APPLE CASSEROLE

1/2 cup butter *or* margarine,
    divided
6 medium sweet potatoes,
    peeled and sliced, *divided*
1/2 cup packed brown sugar
1/2 cup broken pecans
4 large apples, cored and sliced

Use a little of the butter to grease a 13- in. x 9-in. x 2-in. baking pan. Arrange half of the sweet potatoes in pan. Sprinkle sugar and pecans over potatoes and dot with remaining butter. Arrange apples on top of sugar mixture and top with remaining sweet potato slices. Cover tightly with foil and bake at 375° for 1 hour or until potatoes are tender. Stir before serving. **Yield:** 8-10 servings.

OLD-FASHIONED BUTTERMILK CAKE

1 cup butter, softened
2 cups sugar
4 eggs
3 cups all-purpose flour
2 teaspoons baking powder
1/2 teaspoon salt
1/2 teaspoon baking soda
1 cup buttermilk
1 teaspoon vanilla extract

In a mixing bowl, cream butter and sugar with mixer on high until fluffy. Add eggs, one at a time, beating well after each. Sift flour, baking powder, salt and soda; add alternately with buttermilk to creamed mixture, beginning and ending with flour. Add vanilla. Pour into three greased and floured 8-in. cake pans. Bake at 375° for 20 minutes or until toothpick inserted in center comes out clean. Cool cakes completely before icing. **Yield:** 3 8-inch layers.

PINEAPPLE CREME CAKE

1 Old-Fashioned Buttermilk Cake
    (recipe above)
1 can (20 ounces) crushed
    pineapple, undrained
1/3 cup sugar
CREAM CHEESE ICING:
1/4 cup butter *or* margarine,
    softened
1 package (8 ounces) cream
    cheese, softened
1 box (16 ounces)
    confectioners' sugar
1 teaspoon vanilla extract

Make cake and set aside. Combine pineapple and sugar in a saucepan and boil for 5-7 minutes, stirring to prevent sticking. Filling should be slightly thickened and syrupy. Set aside to cool. Pierce top of one cake layer with fork; spread with 1/3 of the filling. Allow to sit 15 minutes. Meanwhile, beat together icing ingredients. Spread thin layer of icing over pineapple filling. Repeat with other layers. Frost sides with remaining icing. Cover tightly and refrigerate several hours or overnight. Allow to reach room temperature before serving. **Yield:** 12 servings.

F or a supper that says "sincerely yours", treat your loved ones to cherished recipes from the heart. Start the meal with refreshing Mixed Greens with Blue Cheese Dressing, along with pleasantly tart Cranberry Muffins. Savor the creamy sauce on the Saucy Chicken Casserole, then satisfy sweet tooths with several of Mom's Soft Sugar Cookies!

TO SERVE WITH LOVE. Clockwise from top: **Mom's Soft Sugar Cookies**, **Mixed Greens with Blue Cheese Dressing**, **Cranberry Muffins**, **Saucy Chicken Casserole**. All recipes on page 27.

Special gatherings deserve extra-special food…like the hearty spread pictured above!

If you're cooking for a crowd, these buffet-style dishes will bring family and friends back for "seconds". Get the conversation rolling with the Pineapple Pecan Cheese Ball, then enjoy Hot Italian Roast Beef Sandwiches with Grandma's Potato Salad. For a delightful dessert, serve slices of luscious California Lemon Pound Cake.

MEMORIES IN THE MAKING. Clockwise from top: **California Lemon Pound Cake** (p. 28), **Pineapple Pecan Cheese Ball** (p. 28), **Hot Italian Roast Beef Sandwiches** (p. 28), **Grandma's Potato Salad** (p. 27).

Wilma Beller
Hamilton, Ohio

Whenever there's an opportunity for a neighborly gesture, this "Best Cook" is there—with a gift from her kitchen!

Wilma Beller of Hamilton, Ohio always keeps delicious treats in her freezer—especially small loaves of zucchini and date nut bread.

"On the spur of the moment, she has something to take to neighbors, friends or co-workers to say 'welcome' or 'congratulations', or as a token of sympathy," says friend Shirley Hill, who nominated Wilma.

"She's a very gracious lady," Shirley adds. "I've had the privilege of knowing her for 25 years. I've eaten in her home many times, and every time I have come away with a wonderful new recipe."

Wilma credited her mother with passing on her strong love of cooking. "My mother was a great cook," she said. "I learned most of what I know about cooking from her."

A busy schedule prevents Wilma, who works as a full-time secretary in a hospital, from cooking as often as she'd like. She enjoys preparing meals for her husband, Gene, but has had to alter her recipes to accommodate his low-cholesterol needs. "I've learned methods of low-sodium and low-fat cooking," she says. (See her Breakfast Granola recipe below.)

Wilma's greatest satisfaction in cooking comes from "seeing someone enjoy a meal I've prepared".

Each month, she gathers with friends for a covered-dish supper. "Originally this group consisted of girls from high school," observes Wilma. "Nowadays, of course, it includes our husbands. We take turns hosting the group.

"Gathering for a meal provides an opportunity to enjoy good company and good fellowship."

❖❖❖
BREAKFAST GRANOLA

4 cups old-fashioned rolled oats
1 cup chopped nuts
3/4 cup bran cereal
1 cup flaked coconut
1/3 cup honey *or* molasses
1/4 cup vegetable oil
1 teaspoon vanilla extract
1 cup raisins
1 cup chopped dates

Spread rolled oats on a 15-in. x 10-in. baking pan. Toast at 350° for 5 minutes. Stir; toast 5 more minutes. Remove from oven but leave heat on. Toss with nuts, bran and coconut; set aside. In a saucepan, combine honey or molasses with oil. Heat but do not boil. Stir in vanilla; pour over oat mixture and toss well. Return to oven and bake 20-25 minutes, stirring 3 times while baking. Remove from the oven. Add raisins and dates; stir well. Cool. Store in airtight containers. **Yield:** 8 cups.

❖❖❖
CHINESE NOODLE SLAW

1 medium head cabbage, chopped (about 10 cups)
5 green onions with tops, chopped
2 packages (3 ounces *each*) Ramen noodles
1/2 cup butter *or* margarine
1 tablespoon sesame seeds
1/2 cup slivered almonds
DRESSING:
1/2 cup vegetable oil
1 tablespoon soy sauce
1/3 cup sugar
1/4 cup vinegar

In a large bowl, combine cabbage and onions. Chill. Meanwhile, break the noodles into small pieces (save the seasoning packets for another use). In a saucepan, melt butter over medium-low heat; brown noodles, sesame seeds and almonds, stirring frequently. Drain on paper towels; keep at room temperature. Combine all dressing ingredients in a mixing bowl; blend with a wire whisk. Twenty minutes before serving, toss noodle mixture with cabbage and onions. Pour dressing over and toss well. **Yield:** 10 servings.

❖❖❖
FRESH PEACH CRISP

6 fresh peaches (about 1-1/2 pounds), sliced
1/4 cup sugar
2 teaspoons lemon juice
1/8 teaspoon almond extract
3/4 cup all-purpose flour
3/4 cup packed brown sugar
1/4 teaspoon salt
1/3 cup butter *or* margarine

Arrange peaches in a lightly greased 2-qt. baking dish. Combine sugar, lemon juice and almond extract; drizzle over peaches. In a small mixing bowl, combine flour, brown sugar and salt; cut in butter with a pastry blender until mixture is crumbly. Sprinkle over the peaches. Bake, uncovered, at 350° for 40-50 minutes or until peaches are tender. **Yield:** 8 servings.

❖❖❖
PERFECT APPLE PIE

2 cups all-purpose flour
2 teaspoons sugar
1-1/4 teaspoons salt
2/3 cup vegetable oil
3 tablespoons milk
6 to 7 tart baking apples
3/4 to 1 cup sugar
2 tablespoons all-purpose flour
1/2 to 1 teaspoon ground cinnamon
Dash ground nutmeg
Dash salt
2 tablespoons butter *or* margarine

In a 9-in. pie plate, sift together flour, sugar and salt. In a measuring cup, whip oil and milk; pour over flour mixture. Mix with a fork until the dry ingredients are moistened. Remove 1/3 cup; press remaining crumbs evenly over the bottom and sides of pie plate. Set aside. Pare, core and slice apples. Combine sugar, flour, cinnamon, nutmeg and salt; toss with apples. Fill the pie crust with apple mixture. Dot with butter. Sprinkle reserved crumbs over apples. Bake at 400° for 50 minutes or until apples are tender and crust is golden. **Yield:** 8 servings.

Quick & Easy Chocolate Treats

WHEN YOU just can't wait to satisfy a craving for something oh-so chocolaty, choose one of these simple sweet treats.

QUICK CHOCOLATE MOUSSE

Elsie Shell, Topeka, Indiana

1 can (14 ounces) sweetened condensed milk
1 package (3.9 ounces) instant chocolate pudding mix
1 cup cold water
1 cup whipping cream, whipped
Additional whipped cream

In a large mixing bowl, combine milk, pudding mix and water. Beat until well mixed. Chill for 5 minutes. Fold in whipped cream. Spoon into individual serving dishes. Garnish with additional whipped cream. **Yield:** 4-6 servings.

HOT CHOCOLATE MIX

Debbie Klejeski, Sturgeon Lake, Minnesota

1 box (8 quarts) nonfat dry milk
1 jar (6 ounces) nondairy coffee creamer
1 container (16 ounces) dry chocolate milk mix
1/2 cup confectioners' sugar

Place all ingredients in a very large bowl or kettle. Stir until well blended. Store in airtight containers or pack into small gift containers. To serve, add 1/4 cup chocolate mix to 2/3 cup hot water. **Yield:** 3 quarts dry mix.

TWO-MINUTE COOKIES

Kerry Bouchard, Shawmut, Montana

1/2 cup butter *or* margarine
1/2 cup milk
2 cups sugar
3 cups dry quick-cooking *or* old-fashioned oatmeal
5 tablespoons unsweetened cocoa
1/2 cup raisins, chopped nuts *or* coconut

In a large saucepan, heat butter, milk and sugar. Bring to a boil, stirring occasionally. Boil for 1 minute. Remove from the heat. Stir in oatmeal, cocoa and raisins, nuts or coconut. Drop by tablespoonsful onto waxed paper. Cool. **Yield:** about 3 dozen.

CHOCOLATE PIZZA

Norma Oosting, Holland, Michigan

8 ounces white chocolate, *divided*
8 ounces semisweet chocolate chips
1/2 cup *each* salted peanuts, mini marshmallows, crispy rice cereal, coconut, red and green candied cherries

In a heavy saucepan or top of a double boiler, melt 6 oz. white chocolate and all the chocolate chips. Stir in peanuts, marshmallows and cereal. Pour onto a greased 10-in. pizza pan or a 10-in. circle of cardboard covered with foil. Spread to even out top. Sprinkle with coconut. Top with cherries. Melt the remaining white chocolate; drizzle over pizza. Chill. **Yield:** 16-20 servings.

CHOCOLATE CHERRY CAKE

Lois Valley, Morgan Hill, California

CAKE:
1 package (18.25 ounces) fudge cake mix
1 can (21 ounces) cherry pie filling

PROMPT PIZZAZZ. Please palates with Chocolate Pizza, a speedy, sweet dessert.

2 eggs, beaten
1 teaspoon almond extract
FROSTING:
1 cup sugar
1/3 cup milk
5 tablespoons butter *or* margarine
1 cup semisweet chocolate chips

In a mixing bowl, stir together all cake ingredients. Pour into a greased 13-in. x 9-in. x 2-in. baking pan. Bake at 350° for 30 minutes or until cake tests done. Meanwhile, in a saucepan, mix sugar, milk and butter. Bring to a boil and boil for 1-1/2 minutes. Remove from the heat and stir in chocolate chips until melted. Pour over hot cake. Frosting will harden as it cools. **Yield:** 15-20 servings.

DOUBLE CHOCOLATE BROWNIES

Flo Burtnett, Gage, Oklahoma

1 egg, beaten
1 box (21.5 ounces) fudge brownie mix
1/4 cup vegetable oil
1/4 cup cold coffee
1/4 cup water
1 cup white chocolate chips *or* coarsely chopped almond bark
3/4 cup chopped walnuts

Place egg, brownie mix, oil, coffee and water in a large mixing bowl. Mix with a spoon until just moistened, about 50 strokes. Stir in chocolate and nuts. Spread in a greased 13-in. x 9-in. x 2-in. baking pan. Bake 30 minutes at 350°. Cool in pan. **Yield:** 36 brownies, 2-1/2 in. x 1/2 in. each.

CANDY BAR PIE

Rosalind Hamilton, Iowa, Louisiana

6 chocolate bars with almonds (1.45 ounces *each*)
1 container (8 ounces) frozen whipped topping, thawed
1 tablespoon vanilla extract
1 prepared graham cracker crust (8 *or* 9 inches)
Shaved chocolate, optional

In a double boiler or microwave oven, melt chocolate bars. Quickly fold into the whipped topping. Stir in vanilla. Spoon into pie crust. Garnish with shaved chocolate, if desired. Chill until ready to serve. **Yield:** 6-8 servings.

Whether you're looking for a sweet conclusion to a meal, a scrumptious snack or a spectacular company dessert, consider these chocolate desserts the grand finale.

From homey White Chocolate Cookies to dramatic Chocolate Mocha Torte, each of these delicious treats is worthy of the place of honor at the end of a memorable meal.

NO. 1 CHOCOLATE. Top to bottom: **Chocolate Buttermilk Squares** (p. 28), **Chocolate Mocha Torte** (p. 28), **Chocolate Malt Shoppe Pie** (p. 29), **White Chocolate Cookies** (p. 29).

When your family asks you for a sweet treat, chances are chocolate's the most-hoped-for choice.

Now, you can truly treat those you love to the scrumptious taste of chocolate in a variety of recipes. You'll find rich family favorites, including a few surprises—like Chocolate *Shortbread*—to satisfy sweet tooths for many mouth-watering months to come!

CELEBRATED CHOCOLATE. Clockwise from lower left: **Chocolate Shortbread** (p. 29), **Chocolate Pound Cake** (p. 29), **Chocolate Angel Food Cake** (p. 29), **Milky Way Ice Cream** (p. 30), **Chocolate Cinnamon Doughnuts** (p. 30), **White Chocolate Fudge** (p. 30), **Homemade Fudge Sauce** (p. 30), **Old-Fashioned Chocolate Pudding** (p. 30).

'My Most Memorable Meal'

A recipe box can hold all sorts of treasures, and that's exactly how Colleen Demuth looks at the one she received from her mother.

"Going through its contents brings back all sorts of memories," says Colleen, who lives in the small town of Le Mars, Iowa. "There are recipes from my grandmothers and my parents that were always family favorites, and they're favorites with my family, too!"

Although the size of the Demuth family living at home has dwindled—six of the eight children are married—Colleen says she still enjoys pulling out the much-used recipe box for one of her children's favorites whenever they visit. "Everyone has a favorite, so we're always cooking up some wonderful treat!" she says.

The four recipes featured here make up Colleen's *most memorable meal*. They take her back to her own roots, reviving fond memories of the days when she was growing up in Nebraska.

Colleen's mother would serve meals on Desert Rose china, just as you see it served here. "All four of these recipes are very easy to make," Colleen notes. "Even the rolls are, although anyone who has made bread knows it does take a little more time and effort."

Today, whether she's cooking for her "smaller" family, or for the entire clan when they're all home, Colleen still heads for that timeworn recipe box to cook up her favorite meal.

FROM MOM'S RECIPE BOX. Clockwise from top: **Cauliflower Au Gratin, Hearty Ham Loaf, Strawberry Glaze Pie, Golden Dinner Rolls.** All recipes on page 31.

MIXED GREENS WITH BLUE CHEESE DRESSING
Peggy Hughes, Albany, Kentucky

(PICTURED ON PAGE 19)

✓ This tasty dish uses less sugar, salt and fat. Recipe includes *Diabetic Exchanges*.

1 small head cauliflower, broken into florets
2 quarts mixed salad greens
4 slices red onion, separated into rings
1/4 cup sliced stuffed green olives
BLUE CHEESE DRESSING:
2 ounces blue cheese, crumbled
1/3 cup salad oil
2 tablespoons lemon juice
1/2 teaspoon sugar
1/4 teaspoon salt
2 tablespoons chopped parsley
3 tablespoons chopped green onion

In large salad bowl, combine first four ingredients. Chill until ready to serve. Combine dressing ingredients; toss with greens mixture just before serving. **Yield:** 8 servings. **Diabetic Exchanges:** One serving equals 1/2 meat, 2 vegetable, 2 fat; also, 181 calories, 310 mg sodium, 5 mg cholesterol, 9 gm carbohydrate, 6 gm protein, 13 gm fat.

MOM'S SOFT SUGAR COOKIES
Arnita Schroeder, Hoagland, Indiana

(PICTURED ON PAGE 19)

1-3/4 cups sugar
1 cup butter, softened
3/4 teaspoon salt
4 egg yolks
2 eggs
1 teaspoon baking soda
2 tablespoons hot water
1 cup (8 ounces) sour cream
4 cups all-purpose flour
1 teaspoon baking powder
1/2 teaspoon nutmeg
Granulated *or* colored sugar
Walnut halves, optional

In a large mixing bowl, cream sugar, butter, salt, yolks and whole eggs. Dissolve baking soda in hot water; add, with sour cream, to butter mixture. In a separate bowl, sift together flour, baking powder and nutmeg; add to egg mixture. Dough will be sticky. Cover and chill several hours or overnight. Roll chilled dough on a well-floured surface. Cut into 2-1/2-in. round or decorative shapes. Sprinkle with granulated or colored sugar. Top plain round cookies with a walnut half, if desired. Bake at 350° for 8-10 minutes or until the cookies are set but not browned. Remove cookies to wire rack to cool. **Yield:** about 7-1/2 dozen.

SAUCY CHICKEN CASSEROLE
Jacki Remsberg, La Canada, California

(PICTURED ON PAGE 19)

1 can (10-3/4 ounces) cream of chicken soup, undiluted
1 can (10-3/4 ounces) cream of mushroom soup, undiluted
2 cups (16 ounces) sour cream
3/4 cup dry white wine *or* chicken broth
1/2 medium onion, chopped
1 cup sliced fresh mushrooms
1/2 teaspoon garlic powder
1/2 teaspoon salt
1/2 teaspoon poultry seasoning
1/4 teaspoon ground black pepper
6 boneless chicken breast halves
Cooked noodles *or* rice
Chopped parsley

In a 13-in. x 9-in. x 2-in. baking pan, combine soups, sour cream, wine or broth, onion, mushrooms and seasonings. Arrange chicken on top of sauce. Bake, uncovered, at 350° for 1 hour or until chicken is tender. Serve chicken and sauce over noodles or rice. Garnish with parsley. **Yield:** 6 servings.

CRANBERRY MUFFINS
Dorothy Bateman, Carver, Massachusetts

(PICTURED ON PAGE 19)

1 cup cranberries, quartered
8 tablespoons sugar, *divided*
1-3/4 cups all-purpose flour
2-1/2 teaspoons baking powder
1/4 teaspoon salt
1 egg
3/4 cup milk
1/3 cup cooking oil
1 teaspoon grated lemon peel, optional
Cinnamon-sugar

Sprinkle cranberries with 2 tablespoons sugar; set aside. Sift remaining sugar, flour, baking powder and salt into large mixing bowl. In separate bowl, beat egg, milk and oil. Make a hole in center of dry ingredients; pour in liquid ingredients. Stir only until mixed; do not overmix. Add berries and lemon peel. Fill greased standard or extra-large muffin cups with mixture. Sprinkle tops of muffins with cinnamon-sugar. Bake at 400° about 18 minutes for standard-size muffins or about 22 minutes for extra-large muffins. **Yield:** 12 standard-size or 6 extra-large muffins.

GRANDMA'S POTATO SALAD
Karla Retzer, Grantsburg, Wisconsin

(PICTURED ON PAGE 20)

1-1/2 quarts mayonnaise *or* salad dressing
1/4 cup packed brown sugar
1 tablespoon sugar
1-1/2 teaspoons vanilla extract
1/2 teaspoon prepared mustard
1/2 cup milk
10 pounds salad potatoes, cooked, peeled and cubed
1 dozen hard-cooked eggs, chopped
4 celery stalks, chopped
5 radishes, sliced
1 medium onion, chopped
1/3 cup chopped green pepper
Salt and pepper to taste
Leaf lettuce
Paprika
Chopped parsley

In a large mixing bowl, combine mayonnaise, sugars, vanilla and mustard. Stir in milk. Gently fold in potatoes, eggs, celery, radishes, onion, green pepper, salt and pepper. Chill several hours or overnight. Serve in a bowl lined with lettuce leaves. Sprinkle paprika and parsley on top. **Yield:** 6 quarts.

TOMATO TIP: To keep tomatoes fresh throughout the fall and even into winter, pick them before frost damages them and place them unwrapped into shallow boxes. Store tomatoes in a cool, dark, dry place (under the stairs works well) and sort them every few days. Put near-ripe ones on the windowsill and weed out any showing signs of spoilage.

PINEAPPLE PECAN CHEESE BALL
June Stone, Brewton, Alabama

(PICTURED ON PAGE 20)

2 packages (8 ounces *each*)
  cream cheese, softened to
  room temperature
1 can (8 ounces) crushed
  pineapple, well drained
1/2 cup chopped green pepper
1/2 cup chopped green onions
1 teaspoon lemon pepper
  seasoning
1 teaspoon seasoned salt
2 cups chopped pecans, *divided*
Assorted crackers

In a mixing bowl, whip cream cheese until smooth. Gently stir in pineapple, green pepper, onions, seasonings and 1/2 cup nuts. Turn out onto a sheet of plastic wrap and shape into a ball. Refrigerate several hours or overnight. Before serving, roll cheese ball in remaining nuts. Serve with crackers. **Yield:** 12-14 servings.

HOT ITALIAN ROAST BEEF SANDWICHES
Betty Claycomb, Alverton, Pennsylvania

(PICTURED ON PAGE 20)

 This tasty dish uses less sugar, salt and fat. Recipe includes *Diabetic Exchanges.*

1 tablespoon butter *or* margarine
1 boneless sirloin tip beef roast
  (5 pounds)
1 can (28 ounces) tomatoes
  with juice, cut up
1/3 cup water
1 tablespoon ground thyme
1 to 3 teaspoons crushed dried
  red pepper
1 teaspoon salt
Semi-hard rolls

In a Dutch oven, melt butter over medium heat. Brown roast on all sides. Add remaining ingredients except rolls; cover and simmer until the roast is tender, about 3-1/2 to 4 hours. Add additional water, if necessary, to keep roast simmering in broth. Remove meat from broth and reserve broth. Let the meat stand 20 minutes. Trim any fat and thinly slice meat. When ready to serve, reheat sliced beef in broth. Serve on rolls. **Yield:** about 20 sandwiches. **Diabetic Exchanges:** One serving (without roll) equals 2 lean meat, 1/2 vegetable; also, 129 calories, 244 mg sodium, 49 mg choles-terol, 3 gm carbohydrate, 18 gm protein, 5 gm fat.

CALIFORNIA LEMON POUND CAKE
Richard Killeaney, Spring Valley, California

(PICTURED ON PAGE 23)

1 cup butter *or* margarine
1/2 cup shortening
3 cups sugar
5 eggs
3 cups all-purpose flour
1 teaspoon salt
1/2 teaspoon baking powder
1 cup milk
1 tablespoon lemon extract
1 tablespoon grated lemon peel
GLAZE:
1/4 cup butter *or* margarine,
  softened
1 to 1-1/4 cups confectioners'
  sugar
2 tablespoons lemon juice
1 teaspoon grated lemon peel

In a large mixing bowl, cream butter, shortening and sugar until light and fluffy. Add eggs, one at a time, beating well after each addition. Combine flour, salt and baking powder; gradually add to creamed mixture alternately with the milk. Mix well after each addition. Add lemon extract and peel. Mix on low until blended. Pour into a greased fluted tube pan. Bake at 350° for 70 minutes or until cake tests done. Turn out onto a rack to cool. For glaze, combine all ingredients and drizzle over cooled cake. **Yield:** 22 servings.

CHOCOLATE MOCHA TORTE
Abby Slavings, Buchanan, Michigan

(PICTURED ON PAGE 23)

CAKE:
1/2 cup unsweetened cocoa
1/2 cup boiling water
2-1/2 cups all-purpose flour
1-1/2 teaspoons baking soda
1/2 teaspoon salt
1-3/4 cups sugar
2/3 cup butter *or* margarine
2 eggs
1 teaspoon vanilla extract
1 cup buttermilk
FILLING:
5 tablespoons all-purpose flour
1 cup milk
1 cup sugar
1 cup butter *or* margarine
1/2 teaspoon instant coffee
  granules
2 teaspoons water
1 teaspoon vanilla extract
2 teaspoons unsweetened
  cocoa
1 cup chopped pecans
FROSTING:
1/2 cup shortening
1/4 cup butter *or* margarine
2-1/2 tablespoons evaporated milk
1 tablespoon boiling water
1-1/2 teaspoons vanilla extract
Dash salt
1 pound sifted confectioners'
  sugar, *divided*
Pecan halves, optional

For cake, make a paste of cocoa and water. Cool and set aside. Sift together flour, soda and salt; set aside. In a large mixing bowl, cream the sugar and butter. Add eggs and vanilla. Blend in cocoa mixture. Add flour mixture alternately with the buttermilk. Blend until smooth. Pour into two greased and floured 9-in. cake pans. Bake at 350° for 35 minutes or until cake tests done. Remove from pans and cool on a wire rack. For filling, cook flour and milk in a saucepan over low heat, stirring constantly, until thick. Cool. Meanwhile, cream sugar and butter until light. Dissolve coffee in water; add with vanilla, cocoa and milk mixture to creamed mixture. Beat until fluffy, about 5 minutes. Fold in nuts. Split each cake layer in half. Divide filling into thirds and spread between layers. For frosting, cream shortening and butter. Add milk, water, vanilla, salt and half the sugar. Beat well. Add remaining sugar and beat until smooth and fluffy. Spread over top and sides of cake. Garnish with pecan halves, if desired. **Yield:** about 16 servings.

CHOCOLATE BUTTERMILK SQUARES
Clarice Baker, Stromsburg, Nebraska

(PICTURED ON PAGE 23)

1 cup butter *or* margarine
1/4 cup unsweetened cocoa
1 cup water
2 cups sugar
2 cups all-purpose flour
1/2 teaspoon salt
1/2 cup buttermilk
1 teaspoon baking soda
2 eggs, beaten
1 teaspoon vanilla extract
3 to 4 drops red food coloring,
  optional
FROSTING:
1/2 cup butter *or* margarine
1/4 cup unsweetened cocoa
1/4 cup buttermilk

1 pound confectioners' sugar
1 teaspoon vanilla extract
Dash salt
3/4 cup chopped almonds,
optional

In a saucepan, bring butter, cocoa and water to a boil. Cool. Meanwhile, in a large mixing bowl, combine the sugar, flour and salt. Pour cocoa mixture over dry ingredients. Mix well. Combine buttermilk and baking soda; add to cocoa mixture along with eggs, vanilla and food coloring, if desired. Mix until well combined. Pour into a greased and floured 15-in. x 10-in. x 1-in. baking pan. Bake at 350° for 20 minutes. For frosting, melt butter, cocoa and buttermilk. Stir in sugar, vanilla and salt. Spread over warm cake and top with nuts, if desired. **Yield:** 15 servings.

❖❖❖
CHOCOLATE MALT SHOPPE PIE

Beth Wanek, Little Chute, Wisconsin

(PICTURED ON PAGE 23)

1-1/2 cups chocolate cookie crumbs
1/4 cup butter *or* margarine,
melted
1 pint vanilla ice cream, softened
1/2 cup crushed malted milk balls
2 tablespoons milk, *divided*
3 tablespoons instant
chocolate malted milk powder
3 tablespoons marshmallow
creme topping
1 cup whipping cream
Additional whipped cream
Additional malted milk balls

Combine crumbs and butter. Press into a 9-in. pie pan. Freeze while preparing filling. In a mixing bowl, blend the ice cream, crushed malted milk balls and 1 tablespoon milk. Spoon into crust. Freeze for 1 hour. Meanwhile, blend malted milk powder, marshmallow creme and the remaining milk. Stir in whipping cream; whip until soft peaks form. Spread over ice cream layer. Freeze several hours or overnight. Before serving, garnish with whipped cream and malted milk balls. **Yield:** 6-8 servings.

❖❖❖
WHITE CHOCOLATE COOKIES

Shana Bounds, Magee, Mississippi

(PICTURED ON PAGE 23)

1/2 cup butter *or* margarine
1/2 cup shortening
3/4 cup sugar

1/2 cup packed brown sugar
1 egg
1-3/4 cups all-purpose flour
1 teaspoon baking soda
1/2 teaspoon salt
2 teaspoons vanilla extract
10 ounces white chocolate,
coarsely chopped
1/2 cup coarsely chopped
macadamia nuts, lightly toasted

In a large mixing bowl, cream butter and shortening. Gradually add sugars, beating until light and fluffy. Add egg; mix well. Combine flour, soda and salt; add to creamed mixture. Blend in vanilla. Stir in chocolate and nuts. Cover and chill dough for 1 hour. Drop by heaping tablespoonsful about 3 in. apart on ungreased cookie sheets. Bake at 350° for 12-14 minutes or until lightly browned. Let stand a few minutes before removing cookies to a wire rack to cool. **Yield:** about 2-1/2 dozen.

❖❖❖
CHOCOLATE ANGEL FOOD CAKE

Mary Ann Iverson, Woodville, Wisconsin

(PICTURED ON PAGE 24)

3/4 cup sifted cake flour
1-1/2 cups plus 2 tablespoons
sugar, *divided*
1/4 cup unsweetened cocoa
1-1/2 cups egg whites, room
temperature
1-1/2 teaspoons cream of tartar
1/4 teaspoon salt
1-1/2 teaspoons vanilla extract
CHOCOLATE FLUFF FROSTING:
2 cups whipping cream
1 cup sifted confectioners' sugar
1/2 cup unsweetened cocoa
Dash salt

Sift together flour, 3/4 cup plus 2 tablespoons sugar and cocoa three times. Set aside. In a large mixing bowl, beat egg whites, cream of tartar, salt and vanilla until foamy. Add remaining sugar, 2 tablespoons at a time, beating about 10 seconds after each addition. Continue beating until mixture holds stiff peaks. With a rubber scraper, fold in flour mixture, 3 tablespoons at a time. Mixture will be thick. Spread into a 10-in. angel food pan. Cut through batter with a knife to remove air pockets. Bake at 350° for 40-45 minutes or until the top of cake springs when lightly touched. Immediately invert cake in pan; cool. Run a knife around sides of cake and remove. For frosting, combine all ingredients in a chilled bowl. Beat until thick enough to spread. Frost the entire cake. Chill until ready to serve. **Yield:** 12 servings.

❖❖❖
CHOCOLATE SHORTBREAD

Katherine Both
Rocky Mountain House, Alberta

(PICTURED ON PAGE 24)

1 cup butter *or* margarine
1/3 cup unsweetened cocoa
2/3 cup confectioners' sugar
Dash salt
1-1/2 cups all-purpose flour

In a large mixing bowl, cream butter until light and fluffy. Blend in remaining ingredients. Chill 1 hour. Drop by rounded teaspoonsful 2 in. apart on greased cookie sheets. Bake at 300° for about 20 minutes or until the cookies are set. **Yield:** about 4 dozen.

❖❖❖
CHOCOLATE POUND CAKE

Ann Perry, Sierra Vista, Arizona

(PICTURED ON PAGE 24)

8 milk chocolate bars without
nuts (1.55 ounces *each*)
2 tablespoons water
1/2 cup butter *or* margarine
2 cups sugar
4 eggs
2 teaspoons vanilla extract
2-1/2 cups sifted cake flour
1/2 teaspoon salt
1/4 teaspoon baking soda
1 cup buttermilk
1/2 cup chopped pecans, optional
Confectioners' sugar, optional

In a saucepan, melt chocolate with water over low heat. Mixture will begin to harden. Cream butter and sugar. Add eggs, one at a time, beating well after each addition. Blend in the vanilla and chocolate mixture. Stir together flour, salt and soda; add alternately with buttermilk to creamed mixture. Fold in nuts, if desired. Pour into a greased and floured 10-in. tube pan or fluted tube pan. Bake at 325° for about 1-1/2 hours or until cake tests done when a toothpick inserted in the center comes out clean. Allow cake to stand 10 minutes before removing from pan. Cool on wire rack. Sprinkle with confectioners' sugar, if desired. **Yield:** 12 servings.

WHITE CHOCOLATE FUDGE

Jan Lutz, Stevens Point, Wisconsin

(PICTURED ON PAGE 25)

1 package (8 ounces) cream cheese, softened
4 cups confectioners' sugar
1-1/2 teaspoons vanilla extract
12 ounces white chocolate
3/4 cup chopped pecans

In a mixing bowl, beat cream cheese, sugar and vanilla until smooth. In a double boiler, melt chocolate. Fold into cream cheese mixture with pecans. Spread into a greased 8-in. baking pan. Chill until ready to serve. Cut into squares. **Yield:** about 48 pieces.

CHOCOLATE FIX: Keep some cocoa powder and chocolate-flavored sprinkles or syrup on hand for garnishes.

MILKY WAY ICE CREAM

Jo Groth, Plainfield, Iowa

(PICTURED ON PAGE 25)

16 ounces Milky Way candy bars
1 quart whipping cream, *divided*
4 eggs
1-1/2 quarts milk
1 package (3.4 ounces) instant vanilla pudding mix
1 package (3.9 ounces) instant chocolate fudge pudding mix

In a double boiler, melt candy bars with half the cream. Beat eggs in remaining cream. Whisk into melted chocolate. Cook and stir for 5 minutes. Cool. Beat milk and pudding mixes. Fold into chocolate mixture. Chill several hours or overnight. Freeze in an ice cream freezer according to manufacturer's instructions. **Yield:** about 3 quarts.

CHOCOLATE CINNAMON DOUGHNUTS

Judi Eaker, Chaffee, Missouri

(PICTURED ON PAGE 25)

2 eggs, beaten
1-1/4 cups sugar
1/4 cup vegetable oil
1 teaspoon vanilla extract
4 cups all-purpose flour
1/3 cup unsweetened cocoa
4 teaspoons baking powder
1 teaspoon ground cinnamon
3/4 teaspoon salt
1/4 teaspoon baking soda
3/4 cup buttermilk
Oil *or* shortening for deep-fat frying
GLAZE:
4 cups sifted confectioners' sugar
1 teaspoon vanilla extract
1/2 teaspoon ground cinnamon
6 tablespoons milk

In a mixing bowl, beat eggs. Add sugar and beat until mixture is thick and lemon-colored. Stir in oil and vanilla. In another bowl, combine flour, cocoa, baking powder, cinnamon, salt and soda. Stir into egg mixture alternately with buttermilk. Chill. Divide dough in half and put half in the refrigerator. On a lightly floured board, roll to 1/2-in. thickness. Cut with a 2-1/2-in. floured doughnut cutter. Repeat with remaining dough. Deep-fry in fat heated to 375° for 3 minutes, turning once. Place on paper towels. Combine glaze ingredients and dip tops of warm doughnuts. **Yield:** 2 dozen.

OLD-FASHIONED CHOCOLATE PUDDING

Amber Sampson, Somonauk, Illinois

(PICTURED ON PAGE 25)

2 cups milk
2 tablespoons butter *or* margarine
2 squares (1 ounce *each*) unsweetened chocolate
2/3 cup sugar
1/3 cup all-purpose flour
1/4 teaspoon salt
2 egg yolks, beaten
1/2 teaspoon vanilla extract
Whipped cream, optional

In the top of a double boiler, heat milk, butter and chocolate until the chocolate melts. Chocolate may appear curdled. Combine sugar, flour and salt. Sprinkle over chocolate mixture. *Do not stir.* Cover the mixture and cook on medium-low for 20 minutes. With a spoon, beat mixture until smooth. Quickly add egg yolks; beat well. Cook 2 additional minutes. Remove from the heat and stir in vanilla. Pour into dessert glasses. Serve with whipped cream, if desired. **Yield:** 4 servings.

HOMEMADE FUDGE SAUCE

Trudy DeFelice, Columbia, South Carolina

(PICTURED ON PAGE 25)

1-1/4 cups sugar
1 cup unsweetened cocoa
1/2 teaspoon ground cinnamon
1 cup whipping cream
1/2 cup milk
1/2 cup unsalted butter, cut into 8 pieces
2 teaspoons vanilla extract

In a heavy saucepan, stir together sugar, cocoa and cinnamon. Add cream and milk; mix well. Over medium heat, bring to a boil, stirring constantly. Cook 2 minutes. Remove from the heat; cool 15 minutes. Add butter and stir until melted. Stir in vanilla. Cool to room temperature. Store, covered, in the refrigerator. Stir before serving. **Yield:** 3 cups.

HAVE YOUR "CANDLES" AND EAT 'EM, TOO! Delight your birthday boy or girl with a cake decorated with edible candle holders! Pick up a roll of Life Savers, and you'll find that small candles fit into the centers perfectly.

GERMAN MEATBALLS

Evelyn Kay, Banning, California

1 pound lean ground beef
1 egg, beaten
3/4 cup soft bread crumbs
1-3/4 cups water, *divided*
1/4 cup chopped onion
1/2 teaspoon salt
Dash pepper
2 beef bouillon cubes
1/3 cup packed brown sugar
1/4 cup raisins
2-1/2 teaspoons lemon juice
1/2 cup coarsely ground gingersnaps
Cooked noodles

Combine beef, egg, crumbs, 1/4 cup water, onion, salt and pepper. Shape into 1-1/2-in. balls. Set aside. In a large skillet, bring remaining water to a boil. Add bouillon, sugar, raisins, lemon juice and gingersnaps. Stir until thoroughly combined. Add meatballs to skillet. Simmer, uncovered, about 20 minutes or until meat is no longer pink. Stir occasionally. Serve with noodles. **Yield:** 4 servings. **If Cooking for Two:** Freeze half the recipe to enjoy another time.

MEMORABLE MEAL

The following four recipes come from Colleen Demuth of Le Mars, Iowa (see photo and story on page 26).

◆◆◆
HEARTY HAM LOAF

1-1/2 pounds ground ham
1 pound ground pork
1/8 teaspoon pepper
2 eggs, beaten
1 cup milk
1 cup coarsely crushed soda
   crackers (about 22)
BASTING SAUCE:
1/2 cup packed brown sugar
1 teaspoon dry mustard
2-1/2 tablespoons vinegar
1/4 cup water

Combine first six ingredients; form into an 8-1/2-in. x 4-1/2-in. x 2-1/2-in. loaf. Bake at 350° for about 80 minutes or until thermometer reaches 170°. Meanwhile, combine sauce ingredients in a saucepan; bring to a boil. Boil for 2 minutes. Baste loaf occasionally after first 10 minutes of baking. **Yield:** 10-12 servings.

◆◆◆
CAULIFLOWER AU GRATIN

1 large head cauliflower (about 6 cups)
1/4 cup butter *or* margarine, *divided*
1/2 cup diced onion
1-1/2 cups (6 ounces) shredded cheddar cheese
1 cup (8 ounces) sour cream
1/4 teaspoon salt
1/2 cup dried bread crumbs

Break cauliflower into sections. Cook for 10 minutes in boiling salted water. Drain well. Combine cauliflower with 2 tablespoons butter and onion, cheese, sour cream and salt. Spoon into a 1-1/2-qt. casserole. Melt remaining butter and toss with bread crumbs. Sprinkle over the cauliflower mixture. Bake at 350° for 30 minutes or until heated through. **Yield:** 10-12 servings.

◆◆◆
GOLDEN DINNER ROLLS

2 packages (1/4 ounce *each*) active dry yeast
1 cup warm water (110°-115°)
1/2 cup sugar
1 teaspoon salt
1 cup milk
1/2 cup shortening
3 eggs, beaten
6 to 6-1/2 cups unbleached flour

Soften yeast in warm water. Place sugar and salt in large mixing bowl. Set aside. Heat and stir milk and shortening until shortening melts (120°-130°). Add to mixing bowl along with eggs and yeast mixture. Stir in 1 cup of flour at a time to form a soft dough that can be kneaded. Knead on a lightly floured board until smooth and elastic. Place in a large greased bowl. Cover and let rise in a warm place until doubled, about 1 hour. Punch dough down. Turn out onto a lightly floured surface. Shape into desired rolls or loaves. Place on greased baking sheets or in bread pans. Cover and let rise until nearly doubled, about 30 minutes. Bake rolls at 375° for 15-18 minutes or until golden. Bake loaves at 375° for about 30 minutes or until bread tests done. Remove from pans and cool on wire racks. **Yield:** 36 rolls or 2 loaves.

◆◆◆
STRAWBERRY GLAZE PIE

6 cups fresh whole strawberries, hulled, *divided*
1 cup sugar
3 tablespoons cornstarch
3/4 cup water
Few drops red food coloring, optional
1 pastry shell (9 inches), baked
Whipped cream

Mash 1 cup strawberries; set aside. In a saucepan, combine sugar and cornstarch; stir in water and mashed berries. Bring to a boil, stirring constantly.

Stir in food coloring, if desired. Cook and stir 3 minutes more. Cool for 10 minutes. Spread about 1/3 cup glaze over bottom and sides of pie shell. Halve remaining strawberries; arrange in shell. Spoon remaining glaze over berries. Chill 1-2 hours. Just before serving, garnish with whipped cream. Pie is best served the day it's made. **Yield:** 6-8 servings.

◆◆◆
LUSCIOUS LEMON PIE
Mary Wharton, Shreve, Ohio

1 cup sugar
3 tablespoons cornstarch
Dash salt
1 cup milk
3 egg yolks, slightly beaten
1/3 cup lemon juice
1/4 cup butter
Grated peel of 1 lemon
1 cup (8 ounces) sour cream
1 pastry shell (9 inches), baked
TOPPING:
2/3 cup whipping cream
2 tablespoons confectioners' sugar
1/8 teaspoon almond flavoring, optional

In the top of a double boiler, combine sugar, cornstarch and salt. Stir in milk, egg yolks and lemon juice. Cook and stir over boiling water until thickened and bubbly. Cook and stir 3 minutes longer. Remove from the heat and stir in butter and lemon peel. Cool, stirring occasionally. When mixture is room temperature, stir in sour cream. Pour into shell and refrigerate several hours or overnight. For topping, whip cream until thick; beat in sugar and almond flavoring, if desired. Continue to beat until stiff. Spread or pipe with pastry bag on pie before serving. **Yield:** 6-8 servings.

◆◆◆
CRISP HASH FOR TWO
Flo Burtnett, Gage, Oklahoma

2 tablespoons butter *or* margarine
1 cup diced cooked beef chuck
1 cup diced cooked potato
1 medium onion, diced
1 tablespoon minced parsley
1/2 cup milk
Salt and pepper to taste

In a heavy skillet, melt butter over medium-high heat. Add all remaining ingredients; mix well. Cover; cook until crisp on bottom. Turn and brown other side. Serve immediately. **Yield:** 2 servings.

FIESTA CORN SALAD

Arlene Mawn, Holley, New York

1 can (15-1/4 ounces) whole-kernel corn, drained
1 cup chopped fresh tomato
1 cup chopped peeled cucumber
1/2 cup chopped celery
1/2 cup diced green *or* sweet red pepper
2 green onions, sliced
1/2 cup bottled Italian salad dressing

Combine all ingredients. Chill several hours before serving. **Yield:** 4-6 servings.

CHEESE AND SAUSAGE APPETIZERS

Debbie Hogan, Tsaile, Arizona

1 pound (4 cups) shredded cheddar cheese, room temperature
1/2 pound (1 cup) butter *or* margarine, softened
2 cups all-purpose flour
1/2 teaspoon salt
1/2 teaspoon black *or* cayenne pepper
8 ounces pork sausage, cooked and drained

In large mixing bowl, combine cheese, butter, flour, salt and pepper. Beat with electric mixer on medium-low speed. Stir in cooked sausage. Form dough into 1-in. balls; place on ungreased baking sheet. Bake at 400° for 15-20 minutes or until light golden brown. Serve warm or cold. Store in refrigerator or freezer. **Yield:** about 5-1/2 dozen.

NEW ENGLAND BLUEBERRY COFFEE CAKE

Audrey Thibodeau, Lancaster, New Hampshire

1-1/2 cups all-purpose flour
1/2 cup sugar
1 tablespoon baking powder
1 teaspoon cinnamon
1/2 teaspoon salt
1-1/2 cups fresh blueberries

1 egg
1/2 cup milk
1/4 cup butter *or* margarine, melted
TOPPING:
1/4 cup butter *or* margarine, melted
3/4 cup packed brown sugar
1 tablespoon all-purpose flour
1/2 cup chopped walnuts

In a large mixing bowl, combine flour, sugar, baking powder, cinnamon and salt. Gently fold in blueberries. In a small bowl, whisk together the egg, milk and butter. Add to the flour mixture and stir carefully. Spread into a greased 8-in. x 8-in. baking pan. Combine all topping ingredients and sprinkle over batter. Bake at 425° for 20-25 minutes or until top is light golden brown. Serve warm or at room temperature. **Yield:** 12 servings.

SPINACH SOUFFLE

Jeanie Perez, Fenton, Michigan

2 cups (16 ounces) cottage cheese
3 eggs, beaten
3 packages (10 ounces *each*) frozen spinach, thawed and drained
1-1/2 cups (6 ounces) shredded cheddar cheese, *divided*
1/2 teaspoon salt
Dash nutmeg

In large mixing bowl, combine cottage cheese and eggs. Add spinach, 1-1/4 cups cheddar cheese, salt and nutmeg. Spoon into greased 12-in. x 7-1/2-in. x 2-in. baking pan. Bake at 350° until set, about 45 minutes. Remove from oven. Sprinkle with remaining cheddar cheese and let stand 5 minutes. **Yield:** 6-8 servings.

GREEK CHICKEN SALAD

Donna Smith, Palisade, Colorado

 This tasty dish uses less sugar, salt and fat. Recipe includes *Diabetic Exchanges*.

3 cups cubed cooked chicken
2 medium cucumbers, peeled, seeded and chopped
1 cup crumbled feta cheese
2/3 cup sliced pitted black olives
1/4 cup minced fresh parsley
1 cup mayonnaise
3 garlic cloves, minced
1/2 cup plain yogurt
1 tablespoon dried oregano

Combine the first five ingredients. Set aside. In a small bowl, combine remaining ingredients. Toss with chicken

mixture. Cover and chill for several hours. **Yield:** 7 servings. **Diabetic Exchanges:** One serving (with light mayonnaise) equals 2-1/2 meat, 2 vegetable, 1 fat; also, 288 calories, 566 mg sodium, 80 mg cholesterol, 11 gm carbohydrate, 23 gm protein, 17 gm fat.

COUNTRY RICE SALAD

Arlyn Kramer, El Campo, Texas

✓ This tasty dish uses less sugar, salt and fat. Recipe includes *Diabetic Exchanges*.

DRESSING:
1/2 cup mayonnaise
1/4 cup prepared mustard
2 tablespoons sugar
1 teaspoon vinegar
1/4 teaspoon salt
1/8 teaspoon pepper
1 to 2 tablespoons milk, optional
SALAD:
3 cups cooked rice, chilled
1/4 cup sweet pickle relish
1 jar (2 ounces) chopped pimiento, drained
1/3 cup finely chopped green onions (including tops)
1/4 cup finely chopped green pepper
1/4 cup finely chopped celery
3 hard-cooked eggs, diced
Fresh parsley
Cherry tomatoes

Combine all dressing ingredients except the milk or cream. Set aside. In a large salad bowl, combine all salad ingredients. Pour dressing over rice mixture; stir gently. Add milk if mixture is dry. Chill several hours before serving. Garnish with parsley and cherry tomatoes. **Yield:** 10 servings. **Diabetic Exchanges:** One serving (using light mayonnaise) equals 1 starch, 1 fat, 1/2 vegetable; also, 144 calories, 280 mg sodium, 85 mg cholesterol, 20 gm carbohydrate, 3 gm protein, 5 gm fat.

COMPANY CASSEROLE

Suzann Verdun, Lisle, Illinois

1 package (6 ounces) wild rice, cooked
1 package (10 ounces) frozen chopped broccoli, defrosted
1-1/2 cups cubed cooked chicken
1 cup cubed cooked ham
1 cup (4 ounces) shredded cheddar cheese
1 can (4 ounces) sliced mushrooms, drained
1 cup mayonnaise

1 teaspoon prepared mustard
1/2 to 1 teaspoon curry powder
1 can (10-3/4 ounces) cream of mushroom soup, undiluted
1/4 cup grated Parmesan cheese

In a greased 2-qt. casserole, layer first six ingredients in order listed. Combine mayonnaise, mustard, curry and soup. Spread over casserole. Sprinkle with Parmesan cheese. Bake at 350° for 45-60 minutes or until top is light golden brown. **Yield:** 8 servings.

TUNA SPINACH BRAID
Germaine Stank, Pound, Wisconsin

1 package (10 ounces) frozen chopped spinach, defrosted and well drained
1 can (6-1/2 ounces) tuna, well drained and flaked
1 cup cream-style cottage cheese, well drained
1/2 cup grated Parmesan cheese
2 garlic cloves, minced
1 tube (8 ounces) refrigerated crescent rolls
3 slices (3 ounces) mozzarella *or* provolone cheese
1 egg, beaten
1 tablespoon water

In a mixing bowl, combine spinach, tuna, cottage cheese, Parmesan and garlic. Set aside. Unroll crescent roll dough onto waxed paper; do not separate dough. Press to seal seams and perforations. Cover with another piece of waxed paper. Roll dough to form a 14-in. x 10-in. rectangle. Transfer dough to a 15-in. x 10-in. x 1-in. baking pan, discarding waxed paper. Spread filling down center of dough lengthwise in a 3-1/2-in. strip. Top with sliced cheese. Make cuts in the dough at 1-in. intervals on both long sides of rectangle almost to edge of filling. Fold dough strips diagonally over filling, overlapping strips and alternating from side to side. Top will look braided. Combine egg with water and brush over entire top. Bake at 375° for 18-20 minutes or until golden brown. Cut into slices. Serve warm. **Yield:** 10-12 appetizer or 4-6 main-dish servings.

APPLESAUCE CAKE
Kathie Grenier, Auburn, Maine

1 cup sugar
1/2 cup shortening
1-1/2 cups applesauce
2 tablespoons molasses
2 cups all-purpose flour
1 teaspoon baking soda

1 teaspoon ground cinnamon
1 teaspoon ground cloves
1/2 teaspoon salt
1 cup raisins

In a mixing bowl, cream the sugar and shortening. Beat in applesauce and molasses. Set aside. Sift together flour, baking soda, cinnamon, cloves and salt; gradually add to batter, mixing well to moisten. Stir in raisins. Pour into a greased and floured fluted tube pan. Bake at 350° for 45 minutes or until cake tests done. Cake will not rise to top of pan. After 10 minutes, remove cake from pan and cool on a wire rack. **Yield:** 8-10 servings.

BAKED BEEF STEW
Sue Hecht, Roselle Park, New Jersey

 This tasty dish uses less sugar, salt and fat. Recipe includes *Diabetic Exchanges*.

2 pounds lean beef stew meat, cut into 1-inch cubes
1 cup canned tomatoes, cut up
6 carrots, cut into strips
3 medium potatoes, peeled and quartered
1/2 cup thickly sliced celery
1 medium onion, sliced and separated into rings
3 tablespoons quick-cooking tapioca
1 slice bread, crumbled
1 cup water

In large bowl, combine all ingredients. Spoon into greased 3-qt. casserole. Cover and bake at 325° for 3-1/2 hours. **Yield:** 6 servings. **Diabetic Exchanges:** One serving equals 4 lean meat, 1-1/2 starch, 1 vegetable; also, 356 calories, 241 mg sodium, 97 mg cholesterol, 27 gm carbohydrate, 35 gm protein, 12 gm fat.

CHOCOLATE ZUCCHINI SHEET CAKE
Charlene Gledhill, Richfield, Utah

2 cups sugar
1 cup vegetable oil
3 eggs
2-1/2 cups all-purpose flour
1/4 cup baking cocoa
1 teaspoon baking soda
1/4 teaspoon baking powder
1/4 teaspoon salt
1/2 cup milk
2 cups shredded fresh zucchini
1 tablespoon vanilla extract
FROSTING:
1/2 cup butter *or* margarine

1/4 cup baking cocoa
6 tablespoons evaporated milk
1 pound (4 cups) confectioners' sugar
1 tablespoon vanilla extract

In a large mixing bowl, combine sugar and oil. Add eggs, one at a time, beating well after each addition. Combine flour, cocoa, baking soda, baking powder and salt; gradually add to the egg mixture alternately with the milk. Stir in the zucchini and extract. Pour into a greased 15-in. x 10-in. x 1-in. baking pan. Bake at 375° for 25 minutes or until cake tests done. While cake is baking, combine all frosting ingredients. Mix until smooth. Spread frosting over cake while hot. Cool on wire rack. **Yield:** 20 servings.

CHICKEN AND APRICOT SAUTE
Carolyn Griffin, Macon, Georgia

 This tasty dish uses less sugar, salt and fat. Recipe includes *Diabetic Exchanges*.

1 cup chicken broth
1 tablespoon cornstarch
Pepper to taste
1 tablespoon cooking oil
1 pound boneless chicken breasts, cut into thin strips
3 cups sliced celery
2 garlic cloves, minced
1 can (16 ounces) apricot halves in natural juice, drained
6 ounces fresh *or* frozen snow peas
Cooked rice

Combine broth, cornstarch and pepper. Set aside. In a wok or large skillet, heat oil on high. Add chicken; stir-fry until chicken is no longer pink. Remove from pan. Add celery and garlic; stir-fry until the celery is crisp-tender, about 3 minutes. Stir in broth mixture. Cook, stirring constantly until thick, about 1 minute. Add apricots, peas and cooked chicken. Stir-fry until heated through, about 1-2 minutes. Serve over rice. **Yield:** 6 servings. **Diabetic Exchanges:** One serving without rice equals 2-1/2 lean meat, 1-1/2 vegetable, 1/2 fruit; also, 204 calories, 114 mg sodium, 64 mg cholesterol, 14 gm carbohydrate, 25 gm protein, 5 gm fat.

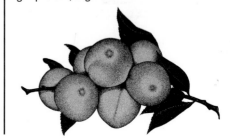

MEAL IN MINUTES

A menu you can make in 30 minutes or less!

As a working mom with a long daily commute, Mary Lee Thomas of Logansport, Indiana became an expert at preparing fast family fare. And now that she's started her own business right at home, "Meals in Minutes" are more important than ever!

"My former job kept me away from home many hours each day," Mary Lee explains. "I'm always here these days…but running my own business is almost as time-consuming! Weekends and holidays are the only times when I can really cook up a storm."

Weekends are when Mary Lee finds time, too, to tend to a good-size garden, work as a literacy volunteer, take an active role in her church, and keep up with her two grown children and four grandchildren. No wonder her hours are still in short supply!

In this speedy meal, Lasagna takes on a whole new twist because Mary Lee makes it in individual rolls.

"While the lasagna is in the oven, I put together a salad with homemade dill dressing. That can marinate until dinner is served. And there's still time to slice a purchased angel food cake and top it with berries and cream for a pretty and tasty dessert."

Whatever your daily schedule, you'll want to give Mary Lee's hearty lasagna a try. Just prepare your family to do some "commuting" of its own—to the kitchen for seconds!

LASAGNA ROLLS

- 6 lasagna noodles
- 1 pound ground beef
- 1 jar (15-1/2 ounces) spaghetti sauce
- 1 teaspoon fennel seeds, optional
- 1 package (8 ounces) shredded mozzarella cheese, *divided*

Cook lasagna noodles according to package directions. Meanwhile, in a skillet, brown beef and drain excess fat. Stir in spaghetti sauce, then fennel seeds, if desired; simmer 5 minutes. Drain noodles. Spread 1/4 cup meat sauce on each noodle; top with 1-2 tablespoons cheese. Carefully roll up each noodle and place, seam side down, in a 9-in. x 9-in. baking dish. Spoon remaining sauce over each roll and sprinkle with remaining cheese. Bake at 400° for 10-15 minutes or until heated through. **Yield:** 6 servings.

DILLED VEGETABLE SALAD

- 1 medium cucumber, peeled and sliced 1/8 inch thick
- 2 medium tomatoes, sliced 1/4 inch thick
- 1 medium sweet onion, thinly sliced
- 2 tablespoons fresh snipped dill *or* 1 teaspoon dried dill weed
- 2 tablespoons salad oil
- 1 tablespoon vinegar
- 2 teaspoons sugar
- 2 teaspoons salt
- 1/4 teaspoon ground white pepper

Place first three ingredients in a bowl. Combine dill, oil, vinegar, sugar, salt and pepper; pour over vegetables and toss. Refrigerate until ready to serve. (Can be prepared the day before, if desired.) **Yield:** 6 servings.

ANGEL FOOD TORTE

- 1 prepared angel food cake
- Red food coloring, optional
- 1 container (16 ounces) frozen whipped topping, defrosted
- 2 cups fresh *or* frozen blueberries, raspberries *or* sliced strawberries

Slice cake into thirds horizontally. If desired, tint the topping pink with a few drops of food coloring. Spread each layer with topping and 1 cup fruit (well drained, if frozen). Reassemble layers and spread remaining topping over entire cake. Chill until ready to serve. **Yield:** 12 servings.

E ntertain a houseful of hungry friends or family with these reliably delicious recipes; they're elegant yet easy to make. Let them help themselves to the eye-appealing ham rolls, munch on mouth-watering muffins and pour the poppy seed dressing over a medley of fruits or greens.

BEST BRUNCH: Honey Poppy Seed Dressing, Orange Cream Cheese Muffins, Best-Ever Asparagus/Ham Rolls. All recipes on page 44.

What better way to celebrate a special day than to spread the table with delicious foods of the season?

Enjoy a hearty entree of Zesty Grilled Chops, cooked over hot coals and seasoned to perfection. Then pass a tray of Marinated Tomatoes and a heaping bowl of Dutch Spinach Salad. And, for a spectacular conclusion, serve Strawberry Cheesecake, loaded with ripe juicy berries.

COUNTRY COOKOUT. Clockwise from top left: **Dutch Spinach Salad**, **Strawberry Cheesecake**, **Zesty Grilled Chops**, **Marinated Tomatoes**. All recipes on page 44.

Maria Goclan
Katy, Texas

It's good to be recognized for your talent, but being the recipient of two big awards on the same day can be a little overwhelming.

That's what happened when we called Maria Goclan of Katy, Texas to tell her she had been selected as a "Best Cook in the Country". During the phone conversation, we learned that earlier that day Maria was named Harris County's (which includes the city of Houston) "Teacher of the Year" for the subject she teaches—English as a second language.

Maria often combines her love of cooking with her lessons at Mayde Creek Elementary School. She feels it helps her students learn to follow directions and gives them a skill which they will use the rest of their lives. Besides, she adds, it's fun.

"It's an excellent way to teach," Maria says. "I give them the recipes and then it's up to them. And you know who makes the best tortillas? Interestingly enough, the boys do. But all the children enjoy making—*and eating*—goodies in my class."

Maria developed her cooking talent at an early age while watching her mother in the kitchen. Her mom, a native of Mexico, didn't have any recipes, so it was "watch and learn" for Maria.

"I learned to season with a little of this and a little of that," she explains.

"When people ask for a recipe, they're usually disappointed to learn that I don't have them written down."

One of her disappointed fans was Rosalie Peters, a former home economics teacher who fell in love with Maria's Spanish Rice (pictured at left).

"It had been a desire all my life to make good Spanish Rice," Rosalie wrote when she nominated Maria for "Best Cook". "So the first time I tasted Maria's rice, I said, 'I've got to have this recipe.' The problem? She didn't have a recipe.

"So Maria invited me over one day, and I watched intently and pinned her down on exactly what she did to this simple little pile of white rice. It worked. And after you make this recipe once, you're hooked!

"I've told many of our friends that if they're ever invited over to Maria's house for a Mexican dinner and they have other plans, change those plans!"

Serve these recipes together for one of Maria's favorite Mexican meals.

❖❖❖
AUTHENTIC SPANISH RICE

- 1 tablespoon bacon drippings
- 3/4 cup long-grain white rice
- 1/2 cup chopped onion
- 1 garlic clove, minced
- 3 small canned tomatoes, diced
- 2 tablespoons tomato juice
- 2 cups hot water
- 1/2 teaspoon salt

In a skillet, heat bacon drippings on medium-high. Add rice; cook and stir until golden brown. Add onion and garlic; stir and cook 3 additional minutes. Add all remaining ingredients. Cook, *uncovered*, on medium heat for 20 minutes, stirring only once after 10 minutes. Check rice for doneness by tasting a few top grains. If rice is firm, add a little water; cover and cook 5 minutes more. **Yield:** 6 servings.

❖❖❖
BEEF FLAUTAS

- 2 pounds beef brisket
- 1 medium onion, cut into fourths
- 1 teaspoon salt
- 1 teaspoon pepper
- 1 teaspoon dried oregano
- 1 teaspoon dried marjoram
Water
- 1 green pepper, finely chopped

18 to 24 corn tortillas
Cooking oil for deep-fat frying
Guacamole, sour cream and salsa, optional

In a Dutch oven, place brisket, onion, spices and enough water to cover. Simmer, covered, about 2-1/2 hours or until meat is very tender. Finely shred beef and chop the onion; mix together with green pepper. Place a spoonful of meat mixture on each tortilla; roll up and secure with toothpicks. Deep-fry flautas in hot oil. Drain on paper towels. If desired, serve with guacamole, salsa and/or sour cream. **Yield:** 9-12 servings.

❖❖❖
MEXICAN-STYLE BEANS

- 1 pound dry pinto *or* black beans, rinsed and drained
- 11 cups water
- 4 bacon slices, cut into small pieces
- 2 garlic cloves, minced
- 1-1/2 teaspoons salt
- 1 onion, chopped
- 1/4 to 1/2 cup fresh cilantro, chopped

In a Dutch oven, combine beans and water. Bring to a boil. Add bacon, garlic and salt. Reduce heat; cover and simmer for 2 hours, stirring occasionally. Add onion and cilantro; continue cooking for about 1 hour or until beans are tender. Drain, reserving cooking liquid. Blend beans in a food processor, using enough reserved liquid to make a smooth but thick mixture. Serve as a dip with tortilla chips or as a side dish with Mexican food. **Yield:** about 6 cups.

❖❖❖
FRESH SALSA

- 2 small fresh jalapeno peppers, seeded
- 1 large tomato
- 1/2 cup lightly packed cilantro leaves
- 2 garlic cloves, minced
Salt to taste

Chop and combine all ingredients. Refrigerate up to 3-4 days. Serve as a dip with chips or use as a relish with main dishes. **Yield:** about 1 cup.

Serve this satisfying combination at your next gathering of good friends or family. To leave more time for visiting, you can prepare the punch ahead of time and assemble the kabobs in the morning, letting them marinate all day before broiling or grilling at dinnertime.

DELICIOUS DUO: Steak and Vegetable Kabobs, Rhubarb Citrus Punch. Both recipes on page 45.

MEAL IN MINUTES

A menu you can make in 30 minutes or less!

Her husband and two teenagers happily help out in the kitchen, making mealtimes quicker and easier for working mom Carol Dalke of Elk Creek, Montana.

"With a new job—and a long commute—I don't have as much time," Carol explains. "Now, my husband cooks more, and the children are pitching in, too. Our son loves to make omelets, while our daughter is putting her 4-H training to good use."

Such kitchen cooperation means Carol still has the time to participate as a 4-H leader and an Extension homemaker, and to enjoy an occasional trip with her family.

Her Minute Steaks Parmesan utilizes a popular cut of meat, prepared with a new twist. "My family loves the Italian sauce and the zesty cheese flavor," she says. "While the steaks are cooking, I prepare the fruit sauce to serve on ice cream for dessert."

Carol continues the meal preparation by tossing the salad ingredients and cooking the corn. "Just before serving, I brush the hot corn with the honey-butter sauce. It's delicious!"

Whether or not you have extra helpers in your kitchen, you'll save cooking time with Carol's meal.

MINUTE STEAKS PARMESAN

    1 egg white, lightly beaten
    2 teaspoons water
Dash pepper
    1/2 cup finely crushed saltine crackers
    1/2 cup grated Parmesan cheese
    4 cube steaks (about 4 ounces *each*)
    2 tablespoons butter *or* margarine
    1 can (8 ounces) pizza sauce

In a shallow bowl, combine egg white, water and pepper. Set aside. On a plate, combine cracker crumbs and cheese. Dip each cube steak into the egg mixture, then coat with cracker/cheese mixture. In a large skillet, melt butter; brown steaks on both sides. Add pizza sauce and simmer for 3-5 minutes. Garnish with remaining crumb mixture. Serve immediately. **Yield:** 4 servings.

ITALIAN SALAD BOWL

    1 bunch leaf lettuce, torn into bite-size pieces
    8 cherry tomatoes, halved
    8 fresh mushrooms, sliced
    4 radishes, sliced
    1 small zucchini, thinly sliced
    1/2 yellow, red *or* green pepper, thinly sliced
    1/4 cup shredded mozzarella cheese
Italian salad dressing to taste

In a large salad bowl, toss all ingredients. Serve immediately. **Yield:** 4 servings.

HONEY BUTTERED CORN

    4 ears fresh *or* frozen corn
    1/3 cup butter *or* margarine
    1 tablespoon honey
    3/4 teaspoon seasoned salt

Cook corn until tender. Meanwhile, melt butter; stir in honey and salt. Brush corn with butter mixture. **Yield:** 4 servings.

PEACH MELBA DESSERT

    2 cups sliced peeled fresh *or* frozen peaches
    2 cups fresh *or* frozen raspberries
    3/4 cup sugar
    2 tablespoons water
Vanilla ice cream

In a saucepan, bring peaches, raspberries, sugar and water to a boil. Reduce heat and simmer 5 minutes. Chill, if desired. Serve over ice cream. **Yield:** about 8 servings.

For food that's full of freshness and flavor, don't forget about asparagus. Those tender little spears are the featured attraction in the tasty recipes on these pages. What variety you'll find: soups, salads, side dishes, suppers—even appetizers and sure-to-please brunch recipes!

DON'T SPARE THE ASPARAGUS! Clockwise from lower left: **Ham and Asparagus Au Gratin** (p. 45), **Asparagus Quiche** (p. 45), **Pasta with Asparagus** (p. 46), **Asparagus, Chicken, Wild Rice Casserole** (p. 46), **Sesame Beef and Asparagus Salad** (p. 46), **Bacon and Asparagus Frittata** (p. 46), **Molded Asparagus Salad** (p. 47), **Asparagus and Tomato Salad** (p. 46).

Savor the flavor of asparagus year-round. Rich in protein, vitamins, minerals—and taste—this vegetable provides a nutritious and delicious accent to any meal. Just look where it's cropped up!

AMAZING ASPARAGUS! Top to bottom: **Asparagus Strata**, **Creamy Asparagus Chowder**, **Asparagus Appetizer Spread**, **Dilly Asparagus**. All recipes on page 47.

THE SEASON for fresh asparagus is short, and you won't want to miss a single spear. These speedy recipes will leave you plenty of time for picking!

CHEESY ASPARAGUS SOUP

Patricia Lockard, Rockford, Michigan

3 pounds fresh asparagus, trimmed
1 small onion, chopped
2 cans (10-3/4 ounces *each*) cream of asparagus soup, undiluted
2 soup cans milk
1 jar (4-1/2 ounces) sliced mushrooms, drained
3 cups (12 ounces) shredded cheddar cheese

In a large kettle, cook asparagus and onion in a small amount of water until tender. Drain liquid. Add all remaining ingredients; heat over medium until the cheese is melted and the soup is hot. **Yield:** 8-10 servings.

WARM ASPARAGUS SALAD

Marcy Fechtig, Burnt Prairie, Illinois

2 cups asparagus pieces
4 slices bacon
1 small red onion, thinly sliced into rings and separated
2 tablespoons vinegar
1 tablespoon sugar
1/2 teaspoon chopped fresh parsley
Salt to taste
1 medium tomato, chopped
1 quart torn mixed greens

Cook the asparagus until crisp-tender. Drain. In a skillet, cook bacon until crisp. Remove to paper towel. In drippings, saute onion until soft; stir in vinegar, sugar, parsley and salt. Stir in asparagus, crumbled bacon and tomato. Pour mixture over mixed greens and toss. Serve immediately. **Yield:** 4 servings.

Microwave: In a 1-qt. dish, microwave asparagus on high 3-5 minutes or until crisp-tender. Drain. Microwave bacon on high until crisp, about 3-5 minutes. Remove bacon. Microwave onion in bacon drippings 2-3 minutes or until soft. Stir in vinegar, sugar, parsley and salt. Stir in asparagus, crumbled bacon and tomato. Toss with mixed greens in salad bowl.

SNAPPY ASPARAGUS DIP

Debra Johnson, Bonney Lake, Washington

1 pound fresh asparagus, trimmed
1 cup (8 ounces) sour cream
1/2 cup salsa (mild, medium *or* hot)
Dash lime juice
Salt and pepper to taste
Dash cayenne pepper

Cook asparagus in a small amount of water until tender. Drain and cool. In a blender or food processor, puree asparagus until smooth. Stir in all the remaining ingredients. Chill. Serve with assorted raw vegetable dippers or tortilla chips. **Yield:** 2 cups.

BREADED ASPARAGUS STICKS

Linda Ordorff, Waverly, Minnesota

2 pounds asparagus spears
1-1/2 cups grated Parmesan cheese
1-1/2 cups fresh bread crumbs
2 eggs, beaten
1/2 teaspoon salt
Dash hot pepper sauce
2 tablespoons butter *or* margarine
2 tablespoons olive oil
Grated Parmesan cheese, optional

Cook the asparagus in a small amount of water until crisp-tender. Drain well. Combine 1-1/2 cups cheese and the

PERFECT PUREE. Serve Snappy Asparagus Dip with your favorite veggies or chips!

bread crumbs on a plate. In a shallow bowl, stir together eggs, salt and pepper sauce. Dip each asparagus spear in egg mixture and roll in crumbs to coat well. Chill 20 minutes. In a skillet, heat butter and oil on medium-high. Brown the spears in a single layer, turning carefully. Remove and keep warm while browning the remaining spears. Serve with additional Parmesan cheese, if desired. **Yield:** 6 side-dish servings.

CHICKEN ASPARAGUS STROGANOFF

Linda Hutten, Hayden, Idaho

1 can (10-3/4 ounces) cream of chicken soup, undiluted
1/4 cup milk
1/4 cup sour cream
2 cups cooked sliced asparagus
1 cup diced cooked chicken
1/4 teaspoon rosemary
1/4 cup shredded cheddar cheese
Cooked rice *or* noodles

Grease a 1-qt. casserole. Combine soup, milk and sour cream. Pour half the soup mixture into the casserole; top with asparagus, chicken and rosemary. Pour remaining soup over chicken. Sprinkle with cheese. Bake at 350° for 30 minutes. Serve with rice or noodles. **Yield:** 4 servings.

ALMOND ASPARAGUS

Helen Manhart, Neola, Iowa

3 tablespoons butter *or* margarine, *divided*
3 tablespoons bread crumbs
1 garlic clove, minced
1/2 teaspoon dill weed
1/2 cup sliced almonds
1/4 cup grated Parmesan cheese
1 pound fresh asparagus, trimmed and cut into 1-inch pieces
1 tablespoon lemon juice

In a skillet, melt 2 tablespoons butter over medium heat. Stir in bread crumbs, garlic and dill; saute until crumbs are golden brown. Remove from heat; stir in the almonds and cheese. Set aside. Cook asparagus in a small amount of water until crisp-tender. Drain; heat with remaining butter. Sprinkle with lemon juice. Spoon asparagus into a serving dish and top with the reserved crumb mixture. **Yield:** 4-6 servings.

BEST-EVER ASPARAGUS/HAM ROLLS
Aida Babbel, Bowen Island, British Columbia

(PICTURED ON PAGE 35)

1-1/2 pounds fresh asparagus, trimmed
16 slices sandwich-type ham
Prepared mustard
6 tablespoons butter *or* margarine
6 tablespoons all-purpose flour
2 cups milk
Salt and pepper to taste
1-1/2 cups (6 ounces) shredded cheddar cheese
6 green onions, thinly sliced, optional

Cook asparagus to crisp-tender. Spread one side of each ham slice with mustard. Roll ham around 2-3 asparagus spears. Layer rolls, seam side down, in a 7-in. x 11-in. baking pan. Set aside. In a saucepan, melt butter over medium heat. Blend in flour to form a paste. Slowly stir in milk, salt and pepper. Cook and stir until sauce is thickened. Stir in cheese and onions, if desired. Pour hot sauce over ham rolls. Cover and bake at 350° for 20 minutes. **Yield:** 8 servings.

HONEY POPPY SEED DRESSING
Abigail Stauffer, Port Trevorton, Pennsylvania

(PICTURED ON PAGE 35)

1/3 cup salad oil
1/4 cup honey
2 tablespoons cider vinegar
2 teaspoons poppy seeds
1/2 teaspoon salt
Fruit sections *or* mixed greens

In a screw-top jar, combine all ingredients except last one. Cover and shake well. Store in the refrigerator until ready to use. Serve over fresh fruit or mixed greens. **Yield:** 3/4 cup.

ORANGE CREAM CHEESE MUFFINS
Ed Toner, Howell, New Jersey

(PICTURED ON PAGE 35)

1 package (3 ounces) cream cheese, softened
1/4 cup sugar
1 egg, beaten
1/2 cup orange juice

1-3/4 cups buttermilk biscuit mix
1/4 cup chopped pecans
6 teaspoons orange marmalade

In a mixing bowl, beat cream cheese and sugar. Add the egg and juice. Beat well. Stir in the biscuit mix only until dry ingredients are moistened. Fold in pecans. Grease six Texas-size or jumbo muffin pans generously. Spoon 1/4 cup batter into each cup. Spoon 1 teaspoon marmalade into the center of each muffin. Divide remaining batter over marmalade. Bake at 400° for 20 minutes or until golden brown. Let stand 5 minutes before removing to a cooling rack. **Yield:** 6 jumbo muffins.

DUTCH SPINACH SALAD
Frances Miller, Baltimore, Maryland

(PICTURED ON PAGE 36)

3 to 4 bacon slices, diced
1 egg, slightly beaten
3 tablespoons sugar
1 tablespoon vinegar
Water
4 cups torn spinach greens
1/2 small onion, chopped
Salt and pepper to taste
Hard-cooked eggs, sliced

In a small frying pan, cook bacon until crisp. Do not drain. In a 1-cup measure, place egg, sugar, vinegar and enough water to make 3/4 cup; pour over bacon and grease. Cook, stirring constantly, until dressing thickens. Season to taste. Pour the hot dressing over greens and onion. Toss; garnish with egg slices. Serve immediately. **Yield:** 4 servings.

MARINATED TOMATOES
Myrtle Matthews, Marietta, Georgia

(PICTURED ON PAGE 36)

 This tasty dish uses less sugar, salt and fat. Recipe includes *Diabetic Exchanges*.

3 large fresh tomatoes, sliced thick
1/3 cup olive oil
1/4 cup red wine vinegar
1 teaspoon salt, optional
1/4 teaspoon pepper
1/2 garlic clove, minced
2 tablespoons chopped onion

1 tablespoon chopped fresh parsley
1 tablespoon chopped fresh basil *or* 1 teaspoon dried basil

Arrange tomatoes in a large shallow dish. Combine remaining ingredients in a jar; cover tightly and shake well. Pour over tomato slices. Cover and refrigerate for several hours. **Yield:** 8 servings. **Diabetic Exchanges:** One serving (without salt) equals 1/2 vegetable, 2 fat; also, 91 calories, 6 mg sodium, 0 mg cholesterol, 3 gm carbohydrate, 1 gm protein, 9 gm fat.

ZESTY GRILLED CHOPS
Blanche Babinski, Minto, North Dakota

(PICTURED ON PAGE 36)

3/4 cup soy sauce
1/4 cup lemon juice
1 tablespoon chili sauce
1 tablespoon brown sugar
1 garlic clove, minced
6 rib *or* loin pork chops (about 1-1/2 inches thick)

Combine the first five ingredients. Place chops in a glass baking dish and pour marinade over. Cover and refrigerate 3-6 hours or overnight. To cook, remove chops from marinade and grill or broil 4 inches from the heat to desired doneness. Brush occasionally with the marinade. **Yield:** 6 servings.

STRAWBERRY CHEESECAKE
L.C. Herschap, Luling, Texas

(PICTURED ON PAGE 36)

CRUST:
3/4 cup ground pecans
3/4 cup graham cracker crumbs
3 tablespoons butter, melted
FILLING:
4 packages (8 ounces *each*) cream cheese, softened
4 eggs
1-1/4 cups sugar
1 tablespoon fresh lemon juice
2 teaspoons vanilla extract
TOPPING:
2 cups (16 ounces) sour cream
1/4 cup sugar
1 teaspoon vanilla extract
STRAWBERRY GLAZE:
1/4 cup water
2 tablespoons cornstarch
1 jar (12 ounces) strawberry jelly

3 tablespoons orange-flavored liqueur *or* lemon juice
Red food coloring, optional
1 quart whole fresh strawberries, hulled

Combine pecans, crumbs and butter. Press into the bottom of a 10-in. springform pan. Set aside. For filling, beat the cream cheese in a large mixing bowl until smooth. Add eggs, sugar, lemon juice and vanilla. Mix thoroughly. Spoon over crust. Bake at 350° for about 50 minutes or until filling is almost set. Remove from the oven and let stand 15 minutes but leave oven on. Meanwhile, prepare topping by combining sour cream, sugar and vanilla. Spread over cake and return to the hot oven for 5 minutes. Cool to room temperature and refrigerate 24 hours. Several hours before serving, prepare glaze: In a saucepan, combine water and cornstarch. Add jelly and cook over medium-high heat, stirring constantly, until jelly melts and the mixture thickens. Remove from the heat; stir in liqueur and food coloring, if desired. Cool to room temperature. Just before serving, loosen and remove sides of springform pan. Arrange strawberries on top of cake with pointed ends up. Spoon glaze over berries, allowing some to drip down sides of cake. Serve immediately. **Yield:** 12 servings.

❖❖❖

STEAK AND VEGETABLE KABOBS
Lorri Cleveland, Kingsville, Ohio

(PICTURED ON PAGE 38)

 This tasty dish uses less sugar, salt and fat. Recipe includes *Diabetic Exchanges.*

1/4 cup vegetable oil
1/4 cup lemon juice
1/4 cup soy sauce
1/4 cup packed brown sugar
2 garlic cloves, minced
3 whole cloves
Dash dried sweet basil
2-1/2 pounds sirloin steak, cut into 1-1/4-inch pieces
2 dozen cherry tomatoes
2 dozen fresh mushroom caps
1 large green *or* sweet red

pepper, cut into 1-1/2-inch cubes
2 small zucchini squash, cut into 1-inch slices
1 medium onion, cut into wedges
Cooked rice

In a bowl, combine first seven ingredients for the marinade. Set aside. Assemble kabobs by threading meat and vegetables on metal skewers. Place in a large glass dish. Pour marinade over kabobs; cover and refrigerate 6 hours or overnight. Turn several times. To cook, grill kabobs over hot coals until the meat and vegetables have reached desired doneness. Remove from the skewers and serve with rice. **Yield:** 10 servings. **Diabetic Exchanges:** One serving equals 2 meat, 1-1/2 vegetable; also, 195 calories, 381 mg sodium, 49 mg cholesterol, 8 gm carbohydrate, 19 gm protein, 10 gm fat.

❖❖❖

RHUBARB CITRUS PUNCH
Ina Frey, St. Clements, Ontario

(PICTURED ON PAGE 38)

8 cups diced rhubarb
5 cups water
1-1/3 cups sugar
2 cups orange juice
3/4 cup lemon juice
1 quart ginger ale, chilled
1 quart fresh *or* frozen strawberries, optional

In a kettle, simmer rhubarb and water until rhubarb is soft. Cool; strain through several layers of cheesecloth. Measure 4 cups juice and return to kettle with the sugar. Heat until sugar is dissolved. Chill. Refrigerate or freeze any remaining rhubarb juice for another batch. Combine sugar/juice mixture with orange and lemon juices. Refrigerate until serving time. Just before serving, add in ginger ale and strawberries, if desired. Pour over ice. **Yield:** about 12 cups.

❖❖❖

HAM AND ASPARAGUS AU GRATIN
Dorothy Pritchett, Wills Point, Texas

(PICTURED ON PAGE 40)

6 slices baked ham
24 asparagus spears, cooked and drained
2 eggs
2 egg yolks
1-1/2 cups heavy cream

Salt and pepper to taste
2 tablespoons shredded Swiss cheese
2 tablespoons grated Parmesan cheese
Finely chopped fresh parsley, optional

Wrap each ham slice around 4 asparagus spears and place, seam side down, in a greased 7-in. x 11-in. baking pan. Beat together eggs, yolks, cream, salt and pepper. Pour over ham rolls. Bake at 350° for about 35 minutes or until top begins to brown and the tip of a knife inserted in the egg mixture comes out clean. Sprinkle with the cheeses and parsley, if desired. Serve immediately. **Yield:** 4-6 servings.

❖❖❖

ASPARAGUS QUICHE
Edna Hoffman, Hebron, Indiana

(PICTURED ON PAGE 40)

1 unbaked pie shell (9 inches)
1/2 pound fresh asparagus, trimmed
2 green onions, thinly sliced
1 tablespoon all-purpose flour
2 cups (8 ounces) shredded Swiss cheese
3 eggs, beaten
1 cup half-and-half cream
1/2 teaspoon salt
1/4 teaspoon basil
1/8 teaspoon cayenne pepper

Bake crust at 425° for 6-7 minutes. Remove from oven and set aside. Cook the asparagus spears in a small amount of water until tender. Drain and cool. Reserve 3 whole spears for garnish; slice the remaining spears into 1/2-in. pieces. Toss together the asparagus pieces, onions and flour. Spread asparagus mixture into crust; sprinkle with cheese. Whisk together eggs, cream, salt, basil and cayenne pepper. Pour into crust. Bake at 325° for 25 minutes. Split the reserved asparagus spears lengthwise and arrange, cut side down, in a wheel pattern on top of filling. Bake 5-10 minutes longer or until a knife inserted in center comes out clean. Let stand 10 minutes before cutting. **Yield:** 6 servings.

ALL TIED UP: For convenience, tie serving-size bunches of asparagus stalks together with kitchen twine and cook, covered, in boiling water for 8-12 minutes. Each bunch can be easily lifted from the water—then just snip the twine and serve.

ASPARAGUS AND TOMATO SALAD

Nanci Brewer, San Jose, California

(PICTURED ON PAGE 40)

 This tasty dish uses less sugar, salt and fat. Recipe includes *Diabetic Exchanges*.

1/4 cup water
1/4 teaspoon onion powder
1 pound fresh asparagus, trimmed
8 to 16 lettuce leaves
2 to 3 large tomatoes, sliced
1 ripe avocado, sliced, optional
DRESSING:
1/2 cup mayonnaise
1/2 cup sour cream
2 teaspoons prepared mustard
1 teaspoon catsup
Salt and pepper to taste

Combine the water and onion powder; bring to a boil. Add the asparagus and cook 3-5 minutes or until asparagus is crisp-tender and bright green. Drain; cool to room temperature. Place 1-2 lettuce leaves per serving on a large platter or individual salad plates. Halve the tomato slices and arrange over lettuce. Top tomatoes with spears of asparagus and slices of avocado, if desired. Combine all dressing ingredients; top each salad serving with a generous dollop. **Yield:** 8 servings. **Diabetic Exchanges:** One serving (using light sour cream and mayonnaise) equals 1-1/2 vegetable, 1 fat; also, 96 calories, 134 mg sodium, 9 mg cholesterol, 9 gm carbohydrate, 3 gm protein, 6 gm fat.

PASTA WITH ASPARAGUS

Barbara Calhoun, Marquette Heights, Illinois

(PICTURED ON PAGE 40)

2 pounds fresh asparagus, sliced diagonally into 1-inch pieces
1 pound very thin spaghetti
8 slices bacon, cut into 1-inch pieces
1/2 cup sliced green onion
1/2 teaspoon black pepper
1/4 cup butter *or* margarine, softened

1/2 cup light cream
1/2 to 3/4 cup grated Parmesan cheese

Cook asparagus in boiling salted water 3 minutes. Drain and set aside. Cook spaghetti according to package directions. Drain and return to kettle to keep warm. Meanwhile, in a skillet, cook bacon until crisp. Remove to a paper towel. In bacon drippings, saute onion until soft. Add asparagus and pepper; heat through. Quickly toss together spaghetti, asparagus mixture, bacon, butter, cream and cheese. Serve immediately. **Yield:** 6-8 servings.

ASPARAGUS, CHICKEN, WILD RICE CASSEROLE

Mary Drache, Roseville, Minnesota

(PICTURED ON PAGE 41)

1 cup uncooked wild rice, rinsed
2 cups chicken broth
1 can (4 ounces) mushrooms with liquid
2 tablespoons butter *or* margarine
6 boneless chicken breast halves
1/2 package onion soup mix
1 can (10-3/4 ounces) cream of mushroom soup, undiluted
1-1/2 pounds fresh asparagus, trimmed
1/4 cup butter *or* margarine, melted
Paprika

Spread rice in a 7-in. x 11-in. baking pan. Add the chicken broth and mushrooms; dot with 2 tablespoons butter. Place chicken breasts in the center of the baking dish; sprinkle with the onion soup mix. Spoon mushroom soup over all. Bake, uncovered, at 350° for 1 hour. Arrange asparagus around outer edges of baking dish; brush with melted butter and sprinkle with paprika. Bake 15-20 minutes more or until asparagus is tender. **Yield:** 6 servings.

SESAME BEEF AND ASPARAGUS SALAD

Tamara Steeb, Issaquah, Washington

(PICTURED ON PAGE 41)

 This tasty dish uses less sugar, salt and fat. Recipe includes *Diabetic Exchanges*.

1 pound top round steak
4 cups sliced fresh asparagus (cut in 2-inch pieces)
3 tablespoons soy sauce

2 tablespoons sesame oil
1 tablespoon rice wine vinegar
1/2 teaspoon grated gingerroot
Sesame seeds
Lettuce leaves, optional

Broil steak to desired doneness. Cool and cut into thin diagonal strips. Cook asparagus in a small amount of water 30-60 seconds. Drain and cool. Combine beef and asparagus. Blend all remaining ingredients except the sesame seeds and lettuce; pour over beef and asparagus. Sprinkle with sesame seeds and toss lightly. Serve warm or at room temperature—on lettuce leaves, if desired. **Yield:** 6 servings. **Diabetic Exchanges:** One serving equals 2 lean meat, 1-1/2 vegetable, 1/2 fat; also, 179 calories, 696 mg sodium, 48 mg cholesterol, 6 gm carbohydrate, 21 gm protein, 8 gm fat.

BACON AND ASPARAGUS FRITTATA

Gwen Clemon, Soldier, Iowa

(PICTURED ON PAGE 41)

12 ounces bacon
2 cups sliced fresh asparagus (cut in 1/2-inch pieces)
1 cup chopped onion
2 garlic cloves, minced
10 eggs, beaten
1/4 cup minced parsley
1/2 teaspoon seasoned salt
1/4 teaspoon black pepper
1 large tomato, thinly sliced
1 cup (4 ounces) shredded cheddar cheese

Cook bacon until crisp. Drain, reserving 1 tablespoon drippings. In a 9-in. or 10-in. ovenproof skillet, heat reserved drippings on medium-high. Add asparagus, onion and garlic; saute until onion is tender. Crumble bacon and set aside a third for topping. In a large bowl, combine remaining bacon, eggs, parsley, salt and pepper. Pour egg mixture into skillet; stir. Top with tomato slices, cheese and remaining bacon. Cover and cook over medium-low for 10-15 minutes or until eggs are nearly set. Preheat broiler; place skillet 6 in. from heat for 2 minutes or until lightly browned. Serve immediately. **Yield:** 6 servings.

STORING SPEARS: Fresh asparagus stores longer if kept standing, cut side down, in an inch of water in the refrigerator. Use a tall pitcher or large beverage container and replace water as needed.

MOLDED ASPARAGUS SALAD

Bernice Morris, Marshfield, Missouri

(PICTURED ON PAGE 41)

1 cup sliced fresh asparagus
1 can (10-3/4 ounces) cream of asparagus soup, undiluted
1 package (8 ounces) cream cheese, softened
1 package (3 ounces) lemon-flavored gelatin
1 cup boiling water
1/2 teaspoon lemon extract
1/2 cup diced celery
1/2 cup diced green pepper
2 teaspoons minced onion
2 teaspoons minced pimiento
1/2 cup finely chopped pecans
1/2 cup mayonnaise
Celery leaves
Chopped pimiento
Lemon slice

Cook asparagus in a small amount of water. Drain and set aside to cool. In a saucepan, heat soup and cream cheese, stirring until well blended. Dissolve the gelatin in boiling water; add the extract. Cool. Combine gelatin, asparagus, celery, green pepper, onion, minced pimiento, pecans, mayonnaise and soup mixture. Pour into a greased 5- to 6-cup mold. Chill until firm, about 4-6 hours. Unmold; garnish with celery leaves, pimiento pieces and lemon slice. **Yield:** 6-8 servings.

DILLY ASPARAGUS

Margot Foster, Hubbard, Texas

(PICTURED ON PAGE 42)

 This tasty dish uses less sugar, salt and fat. Recipe includes *Diabetic Exchanges.*

1 pound fresh asparagus, trimmed
1 jar (2 ounces) diced pimiento, drained
1/2 cup vinegar
1/4 cup olive oil
1 tablespoon sugar
1 tablespoon chopped fresh parsley
2 teaspoons dried minced onion
1 teaspoon dried dill weed
1/2 teaspoon salt
1/4 teaspoon coarse ground black pepper

Cook the asparagus in a small amount of water until crisp-tender. Drain. In a jar with a tight-fitting lid, combine all the remaining ingredients and shake well. Place asparagus in a shallow dish; pour marinade over asparagus. Cover and refrigerate 8 hours. To serve, remove asparagus and arrange on a platter; remove pimiento and onion from marinade with a slotted spoon and sprinkle over asparagus. **Yield:** 4 servings. **Diabetic Exchanges:** One serving equals 1 vegetable, 1/2 starch, 2-1/2 fat; also, 173 calories, 299 mg sodium, 0 cholesterol, 11 gm carbohydrate, 3 gm protein, 14 gm fat.

CREAMY ASPARAGUS CHOWDER

Shirley Beachum, Shelby, Michigan

(PICTURED ON PAGE 42)

1/4 cup butter *or* margarine
2 medium onions, chopped
2 cups chopped celery
1 garlic clove, minced
1/2 cup all-purpose flour
1 large potato, peeled and cut into 1/2-inch cubes
4 cups milk
4 cups chicken broth
1/2 teaspoon dried thyme
1/2 teaspoon dried marjoram
4 cups chopped fresh asparagus, cooked and drained
Salt and pepper to taste
Sliced almonds
Shredded cheddar cheese
Chopped fresh tomato

In a Dutch oven, melt butter; saute onions, celery and garlic until tender. Stir in flour. Add potato, milk, broth and herbs; cook over low heat, stirring occasionally, until the potato is tender and soup is thickened, about 20-30 minutes. Add asparagus, salt and pepper; heat through. To serve, sprinkle with almonds, cheese and the chopped tomato. **Yield:** about 2-1/2 quarts.

ASPARAGUS STRATA

Ethel Pressel, New Oxford, Pennsylvania

(PICTURED ON PAGE 42)

12 slices white bread
12 ounces sharp process cheese, diced
1-1/2 pounds fresh asparagus, trimmed
2 cups diced cooked ham
6 eggs
3 cups milk
2 tablespoons minced onion
1/2 teaspoon salt
1/4 teaspoon dry mustard

Using a doughnut cutter, cut 12 circles and holes from bread; set aside. Tear remaining bread in pieces and place in a greased 13-in. x 9-in. x 2-in. baking pan. Layer cheese, asparagus and ham over torn bread; arrange bread circles and holes on top. Lightly beat eggs with milk. Add onion, salt and mustard; mix well. Pour egg mixture over bread circles and holes. Cover and refrigerate at least 6 hours or overnight. Bake, uncovered, at 325° for 55 minutes or until top is light golden brown. Let stand 10 minutes before serving. **Yield:** 6-8 servings.

ASPARAGUS APPETIZER SPREAD

Linda Stotts, Lowell, Ohio

(PICTURED ON PAGE 42)

1 pound fresh asparagus, trimmed
1-1/2 cups (12 ounces) sour cream, *divided*
1 package (8 ounces) cream cheese, softened
1 envelope unflavored gelatin
1 cup finely chopped cooked ham
1 tablespoon chopped chives
1/2 teaspoon seasoned salt
1/8 teaspoon black pepper
Assorted crackers

Cook asparagus in a small amount of water until tender. Drain, reserving 1/4 cup liquid. Cool. Puree asparagus until smooth. Add 1 cup sour cream and the cream cheese; blend well. In a saucepan, combine gelatin and reserved liquid; heat slowly until the gelatin is dissolved. Remove from the heat; stir in the asparagus mixture, ham, chives, salt and pepper. Pour into a greased 1-qt. round-bottom bowl. Cover and chill until set, about 6 hours. Unmold onto a plate and spread with reserved sour cream. Garnish with additional chopped ham and cooked asparagus, if desired. Serve with crackers. **Yield:** 6-8 servings.

SPEEDY SOUP: To make a quick cream of asparagus soup, chop and cook asparagus spears until tender. Drain the liquid and add a can of ready-to-serve cream of mushroom or chicken soup. Garnish with fried crumbled bacon. Voila!

❖You can also save the tough ends of asparagus spears for soup. Simmer them until tender, then puree in a blender or food processor until smooth.

47

SUMMER STUFFED PEPPERS

Pat Whitaker, Lebanon, Oregon

 This tasty dish uses less sugar, salt and fat. Recipe includes *Diabetic Exchanges*.

8 medium yellow, green *or* sweet red peppers
1-1/2 pounds lean ground beef
1/2 garlic clove, minced
1 medium onion, minced
1/2 cup finely chopped cabbage
1 medium carrot, shredded
1/2 cup shredded zucchini
1 can (28 ounces) tomatoes with liquid, cut up
1/2 cup uncooked long-grain rice
1 tablespoon brown sugar
1/4 teaspoon dried basil
Pepper to taste

Cut the tops off each pepper and reserve. Cook peppers in boiling water until crisp-tender, about 2-3 minutes. Remove from water and rinse with cold water. Remove stems from pepper tops and chop enough of the tops to make 1/3 cup. In a large skillet, brown ground beef over medium heat. Add garlic, onion, cabbage, carrot, zucchini and reserved chopped peppers. Saute until vegetables are tender. Add tomatoes, rice, sugar, basil and pepper. Cover and reduce heat to simmer. Cook until the rice is tender, about 20 minutes. Stuff hot meat mixture into peppers. Serve immediately. **Yield:** 8 servings. **Diabetic Exchanges:** One serving equals 3 lean meat, 2 vegetable, 1 starch, 1/2 fat; also, 315 calories, 234 mg sodium, 67 mg cholesterol, 25 gm carbohydrate, 28 gm protein, 12 gm fat.

POOR MAN'S FILET MIGNON

Gayle Mollenkamp, Russell Springs, Kansas

2 pounds extra-lean ground beef
4 slices bread, crumbed
2 eggs, beaten
1/2 cup milk
2 teaspoons salt
1 tablespoon minced onion
2 teaspoons dried celery flakes
1/2 teaspoon chili powder
1 bottle (18 ounces) smoke-flavored barbecue sauce, *divided*
12 slices uncooked bacon

Combine first eight ingredients and 2 tablespoons barbecue sauce. Form into 12 thick patties. Wrap a bacon slice around the sides of each patty and se-

cure with a toothpick. Bake on a rack at 350° for 50-60 minutes or until desired doneness is reached. Baste frequently with remaining barbecue sauce the last 30 minutes. **Yield:** 12 servings.

OATMEAL CHOCOLATE CHIP CAKE

Luanne Thomson, Mannheim, Germany

1-3/4 cups boiling water
1 cup uncooked oatmeal
1 cup packed brown sugar
1 cup sugar
1/2 cup butter *or* margarine, softened
3 eggs
1-3/4 cups all-purpose flour
1 teaspoon baking soda
1 tablespoon baking cocoa
1/4 teaspoon salt
1 package (12 ounces) chocolate chips, *divided*
3/4 cup chopped walnuts

In a mixing bowl, pour water over oatmeal. Allow to stand 10 minutes. Add sugars and butter, stirring until the butter melts. Add eggs, one at a time, mixing well after each addition. Sift flour, soda, cocoa and salt together. Add to batter. Mix well. Stir in half the chocolate chips. Pour into a greased 13-in. x 9-in. x 2-in. baking pan. Sprinkle top of cake with walnuts and remaining chips. Bake at 350° for about 40 minutes. **Yield:** 12 servings.

APRICOT MUFFINS

Ann Chamberlain, Denver, Colorado

1 cup dried apricots, cut up
1 cup boiling water
1/2 cup butter *or* margarine
1 cup sugar
3/4 cup sour cream
2 cups all-purpose flour
1 teaspoon baking soda
1/2 teaspoon salt
1 tablespoon grated orange peel
1/2 cup chopped nuts
TOPPING:
1/4 cup sugar
1/4 cup orange juice

In a small bowl, combine apricots and water. Let stand 5 minutes. Drain well and set aside. In a large mixing bowl, cream butter and sugar until fluffy. Add sour cream and mix well. Combine dry ingredients and add to butter mixture. Mix on low only until combined. Fold in orange peel, nuts and apricots. Batter will be very stiff. Spoon into well-

greased muffin tins, filling each cup almost to the top. Bake at 400° for 18-20 minutes or until done. Combine sugar and orange juice; dip tops of warm muffins in mixture. **Yield:** 12 muffins.

FRUIT PIZZA

Doris Sather, Eleva, Wisconsin

CRUST:
1/2 cup butter *or* margarine
1/2 cup vegetable shortening
1 cup sugar
1 egg
1 teaspoon vanilla extract
2 cups all-purpose flour
1/2 teaspoon cream of tartar
1/2 teaspoon baking soda
1/4 teaspoon salt
CREAM FILLING:
2 packages (8 ounces *each*) cream cheese, softened
1 cup confectioners' sugar
1 carton (8 ounces) frozen whipped topping, thawed
GLAZE:
1 cup pineapple juice
1 cup orange juice
2 tablespoons cornstarch
1-1/2 cups fresh raspberries
2 kiwifruit, peeled and sliced
2 bananas, sliced
1 pint fresh strawberries, hulled and sliced

In a mixing bowl, cream butter, shortening and sugar. Add egg and vanilla. Combine dry ingredients; blend into creamed mixture. Press dough into a 14- or 16-in. pizza pan. Bake at 350° 8-10 minutes or until light golden brown. Cool. For the filling, whip cream cheese until smooth; add sugar and whipped topping. Spread over crust. For glaze, combine juices with cornstarch; cook and stir until thickened. Reserve 1/2 cup; spread remaining warm glaze over filling. Arrange fruit over glaze and brush reserved glaze over fruit. Chill until ready to serve. (Note: If making a day ahead, substitute another seasonal fruit for bananas.) **Yield:** 12 servings.

MARINATED MUSHROOMS

Agnes Smith, Bristol, Maine

1 pound fresh mushrooms
1/2 cup sliced green onions
1/4 cup chopped sweet red pepper
2 tablespoons minced fresh parsley
1 bottle (8 ounces) Italian salad dressing

In a glass bowl, combine all ingredients and allow to marinate several hours or overnight. **Yield:** 6 servings.

MANDARIN ALMOND SALAD

Doreena Becker, Bellevue, Washington

1/2 cup sliced almonds
3 tablespoons sugar
1 bunch red leaf lettuce, torn in bite-size pieces
1 small red onion, chopped
1 can (11 ounces) mandarin oranges, drained or 4 mandarin oranges, sectioned
DRESSING:
1/2 teaspoon salt
Dash pepper
1/4 cup vegetable oil
1 tablespoon chopped parsley
2 tablespoons sugar
2 tablespoons vinegar
Dash hot pepper sauce

In a small skillet, heat the almonds and sugar over low. Cook and stir constantly until almonds are coated with a sugar glaze. Remove and allow to cool. Meanwhile, combine all dressing ingredients and set aside. Just before serving, toss lettuce, onion and oranges with the dressing and almonds. **Yield:** 4 servings.

ASPARAGUS ENCHILADAS

Janet Hill, Sacramento, California

1/3 cup cooking oil
1 dozen flour tortillas (8 inches each)
1/2 cup butter or margarine
1/2 cup all-purpose flour
2 cans (15 ounces each) chicken broth
1 cup (8 ounces) sour cream
1/2 cup green taco sauce
3 cups (12 ounces) shredded Monterey Jack cheese, *divided*
3 cups shredded cooked chicken
1/2 cup chopped green onions, *divided*
2 pounds fresh asparagus, trimmed
1/3 cup grated Parmesan cheese
1/4 cup sliced ripe olives

In a skillet, heat oil over medium-high. Soften tortillas in the hot oil 30 seconds per side. Drain on paper towel; cool. In a large saucepan, melt butter over medium heat. Blend in flour.

Whisk in chicken broth; cook and stir until thickened. Remove from the heat. Stir in sour cream and taco sauce. Keep warm but do not boil. Divide the chicken, 2-1/2 cups Monterey Jack cheese and all but 2 tablespoons of the onions over the 12 tortillas. Arrange asparagus over filling with the tips extending beyond the tortillas. Top each with 2 tablespoons sauce. Roll up and arrange, seam side down, in a 13-in. x 9-in. x 2-in. baking pan. Top with reserved sauce and the Parmesan cheese. Bake at 400° for 25 minutes or until bubbly. Sprinkle with remaining Monterey Jack cheese and return to the oven just until melted. Garnish with olives and reserved onions. Serve with additional green taco sauce. **Yield:** 12 servings.

SPICY CHICKEN WINGS

Nonie Dean, Balzac, Alberta

1 can (6 ounces) frozen orange juice concentrate, thawed
1 can (6 ounces) tomato paste
1/4 cup honey or packed brown sugar
2 to 3 garlic cloves, crushed
1 teaspoon grated lime peel
1 teaspoon grated lemon peel
1 teaspoon grated orange peel
2 tablespoons lemon juice
2 tablespoons lime juice
1/2 teaspoon seasoned pepper
1/2 teaspoon salt
1/4 teaspoon thyme
Few drops hot pepper sauce
30 to 36 chicken wings or drumettes (about 3-1/2 pounds)

In a saucepan, combine all ingredients except chicken; heat and stir until blended. Cool to room temperature. Place the chicken in a shallow baking pan; pour sauce over. Cover and let marinate in the refrigerator 12-24 hours. To cook, remove chicken from the marinade and place on a broiler pan. Reserve marinade. Bake at 375° for about 40 minutes or until tender. Turn chicken and brush with marinade occasionally. **Yield:** 6 main-dish or 12 appetizer servings.

TEX-MEX QUICHE

Hazel Turner, Houston, Texas

1 unbaked pie shell (9 inches)
1 teaspoon chili powder
1 cup (4 ounces) shredded cheddar cheese
1 cup (4 ounces) shredded Monterey Jack cheese

1 tablespoon all-purpose flour
3 eggs, beaten
1-1/2 cups half-and-half cream
1 can (4 ounces) chopped green chilies, well drained
1 can (2-1/2 ounces) sliced ripe olives, drained
1 teaspoon salt
1/4 teaspoon pepper

Sprinkle chili powder over the inside of the pie shell. Combine cheeses with flour and place in pie shell. Combine eggs, cream, chilies, olives, salt and pepper. Pour over cheese. Bake at 325° for 45-55 minutes or until a knife inserted in the center comes out clean. Cool for 10 minutes before cutting into wedges. **Yield:** 6 servings.

CHIMICHANGAS

Laura Towns, Glendale, Arizona

1/4 cup bacon grease
2 cups chopped or shredded cooked beef, pork or chicken
1 medium onion, diced
2 garlic cloves, minced
2 medium tomatoes, chopped
2 cans (4 ounces each) chopped green chilies
1 large peeled boiled potato, diced
1 teaspoon salt
1-1/2 teaspoons dried oregano
1 to 2 teaspoons chili powder or to taste
2 tablespoons minced fresh cilantro
12 large flour tortillas, warmed
Vegetable oil
Shredded cheddar cheese
Sour cream
Guacamole
Salsa
Shredded lettuce
Chopped tomatoes
Sliced ripe olives

In a skillet, melt bacon grease over medium heat. Saute meat, onion, garlic, tomatoes, chilies and potatoes until the onion softens. Add salt, oregano, chili powder and cilantro; simmer 2-3 minutes. Place a scant 1/2 cup meat filling on each tortilla. Fold, envelope-style, like a burrito. Fry, seam side down, in 1/2 in. of hot oil (360°-375°) until crispy and brown. Turn and brown other side. Drain briefly on a paper towel. Place on a serving plate and top with shredded cheese, a dollop of sour cream, guacamole and salsa. Place shredded lettuce next to chimichanga and top with tomatoes and olives. Serve immediately. **Yield:** 12 servings.

DOUBLE ORANGE COOKIES

Pamela Kinney, Irving, Texas

1-1/2 cups sugar
1 cup butter *or* margarine, softened
1 cup (8 ounces) sour cream
2 eggs
1 can (6 ounces) orange juice concentrate, thawed, *divided*
4 cups all-purpose flour
1 teaspoon baking powder
1 teaspoon baking soda
1/2 teaspoon salt
2 tablespoons grated orange peel

FROSTING:
1 package (3 ounces) cream cheese, softened
1 tablespoon butter *or* margarine, softened
2 cups confectioners' sugar
1 tablespoon grated orange peel
1 tablespoon reserved orange juice concentrate
2 tablespoons milk

In a large mixing bowl, cream sugar and butter until fluffy. Add sour cream and eggs. Beat until well blended. Reserve 1 tablespoon orange juice concentrate for frosting. Add the remaining concentrate with combined dry ingredients to the creamed mixture; mix well. Stir in orange peel. Drop by rounded tablespoonfuls onto lightly greased cookie sheets. Bake at 350° for about 10 minutes or until edges just begin to brown. Remove from the cookie sheets and allow to cool on a wire rack before frosting. For frosting, combine all ingredients in a small mixing bowl and beat until smooth. Spread a small amount over each cookie. **Yield:** about 7 dozen 2-1/2-inch cookies.

ELEPHANT EARS

Jane Carlorsky, Delton, Michigan

1 package (1/4 ounce) active dry yeast
1/4 cup warm water (110°-115°)
2 cups all-purpose flour
2 tablespoons sugar
1/2 teaspoon salt

1/2 cup butter *or* margarine
1/2 cup warm milk (110°-115°)
1 egg

FILLING:
2 tablespoons butter *or* margarine, softened
1/2 cup sugar
1 teaspoon ground cinnamon

TOPPING:
1-1/2 cups sugar
1 teaspoon cinnamon
1/2 cup chopped walnuts, optional

Dissolve yeast in water. In a large mixing bowl, combine flour, sugar and salt. Cut butter into flour mixture as for pastry. Beat milk, egg and yeast mixture until smooth. Stir into the flour mixture and shape into a ball. Place in a greased bowl; cover and chill for at least 2 hours. Turn out onto a floured board; punch dough down. Cover with a towel and allow to rest 10 minutes. Roll into a 18-in. x 10-in. rectangle. Spread with softened butter. Combine remaining filling ingredients and sprinkle over butter. Starting with the long side, roll up dough jelly-roll style and pinch the edges to seal. Cut into 1-in. slices. Mix the topping ingredients and sprinkle a portion of the mixture on waxed paper. Place one slice of dough on top of the mixture and roll to a 5-in. circle, turning to coat both sides. Place on greased baking sheets. Repeat until all the circles are rolled and coated. Sprinkle tops of ears with leftover topping, if desired. Bake at 375° for 10-12 minutes or until golden brown. Cool on wire racks. **Yield:** 1-1/2 dozen.

COUNTRY POPPY SEED CAKE

Laurie Mace, Los Osos, California

1/4 cup poppy seeds
1 package (5-1/4 ounces) instant vanilla pudding mix
1 package (18-1/4 ounces) white cake mix (without pudding)
1/2 cup vegetable oil
4 eggs
1 cup water
1 teaspoon almond extract
2 tablespoons sugar
1/2 teaspoon ground cinnamon

GLAZE:
1/2 cup confectioners' sugar
1/4 teaspoon vanilla extract
1 to 2 teaspoons milk

In a large mixing bowl, combine poppy seeds, pudding and cake mix. Add oil, eggs, water and almond extract. Blend with an electric mixer on low speed until dry ingredients are moistened. Increase speed to medium and mix for 2 minutes. Combine sugar and cinna-

mon; sprinkle into a greased fluted tube pan. Pour batter into pan and bake at 325° for about 1 hour or until cake tests done. Allow cake to cool 10 minutes before removing to a cooling rack. Combine glaze ingredients and drizzle over cooled cake. **Yield:** 12-16 servings.

GARDEN-FRESH TOMATO SOUP

Charlotte Goldbery, Honey Grove, Pennsylvania

1/2 cup butter *or* margarine
2 tablespoons olive oil
1 large onion, sliced
2 sprigs fresh thyme *or* 1/2 teaspoon dried thyme
4 fresh basil leaves *or* 1/2 teaspoon dried basil
1 teaspoon salt
1/4 teaspoon freshly ground black pepper
2-1/2 pounds diced fresh ripe tomatoes *or* 2 cans (16 ounces each) Italian-style tomatoes with juice
3 tablespoons tomato paste
1/4 cup all-purpose flour
3-3/4 cups chicken broth, *divided*
1 teaspoon sugar
1 cup heavy cream

CROUTONS:
8 slices day-old French *or* Italian bread
1 large garlic clove, sliced lengthwise
2 tablespoons olive oil

In a large kettle, heat butter and olive oil over medium-high. Add onions and seasonings. Cook, stirring occasionally, until the onion is soft. Add the tomatoes and paste. Stir to blend. Simmer 10 minutes. Place the flour in a small mixing bowl and stir in 1/4 cup chicken broth. Stir into the tomato mixture. Add the remaining broth. Simmer 30 minutes, stirring frequently. Allow mixture to cool and run through a sieve, food mill or food processor. Return the pureed mixture to the kettle. Add the sugar and cream. Heat through, stirring occasionally. To prepare the croutons, rub the garlic over both sides of the bread. Brush with olive oil and place on a baking sheet. Bake at 350° for 10-12 minutes or until toasted. Turn and toast other side 2-3 minutes. Just before serving, top each bowl with one crouton. **Yield:** 8 servings.

Feast your eyes on this irresistible dessert…crunchy chocolate waffles crowned by a scoop of ice cream, fresh raspberries and rivulets of warmed chocolate sauce. One taste and you'll agree—waffles aren't just for breakfast anymore!

LOVE AT FIRST BITE: Chocolate Dessert Waffles (recipe on p. 59).

For a great-tasting get-together with family or friends, treat them to the recipes shown above.

Fire up the grill (or get the broiler going) for a hearty sandwich of Speidis with a side dish of spicy Zucchini Harvest Salad. You'll love the herb-topped Parmesan Potato Rounds, guaranteed to steal the show. And, for a beautiful conclusion, try the Cherry Berry Pie. It's just like Mom used to make!

FAMILY FARE. Clockwise from top: **Speidis, Cherry Berry Pie, Zucchini Harvest Salad, Parmesan Potato Rounds**. All recipes on page 59.

Best Cook

Marietta Saladin
Woodstock, Illinois

Autumn is a special time for this "Best Cook". It's the time when Marietta Saladin of Woodstock, Illinois can get back in the kitchen and do some cooking!

"When it's so hot and humid during the summer, the last place I want to be is in the kitchen," Marietta says. "But when fall rolls around, I really enjoy cooking a hearty meal."

Glazed Apple Cookies (pictured above) are one of her favorite fall treats. She's had the recipe for years, and it's still requested often—year-round!

"I've had that recipe since my first child was little, so I've used it a long time," she says. "It was always one of the kids' favorites, and now it's a favorite of my grandchildren. I like to use Jonathan apples in the recipe, since that's my favorite type of apple."

Learned from Mother

Marietta learned to cook from her mother and picked up many recipes from her.

"I would always watch my mother, who was a good German cook," Marietta explains. "If she was going to be out of town, she'd tell me what to make while she was gone. That was my first cooking experience."

Marietta grew up on a farm near Woodstock, but it wasn't the typical Midwest farm with cows, corn and chickens. Her family operated one of the nation's largest rose farms,

providing millions of long-stemmed beauties to the wholesale market in Chicago.

"Our farm was *huge* and oh, so pretty," she remembers. "But when World War II came, my father had to raise tomatoes to help the effort. So we went from red roses to red tomatoes!"

Marietta also picked up cooking skills from her mother-in-law, who operated a boarding house in the Upper Peninsula of Michigan.

"I learned how to make chicken and polenta from her, and it's still a family favorite," Marietta says. "If any member of the family knows I'm making it, they seem to find their way over here just in time to eat."

She was nominated for "Best Cook" by her daughter Gretchen and daughter-in-law Lisa.

"Even now, with all the kids grown and married and with children of their own, Mom's table is a very special place," Gretchen says. "Mom always believed that a healthy, wholesome meal at the end of the day was a must for a happy family."

Marietta enjoys fall cooking best, but the recipes she shares here are delicious anytime of year!

GLAZED APPLE COOKIES

 1/2 cup shortening
1-1/2 cups packed brown sugar
 1 teaspoon baking soda
 1 teaspoon salt
 1 teaspoon ground cinnamon
 1 teaspoon ground cloves
 1/2 teaspoon ground nutmeg
 1 egg, beaten
 1 cup finely chopped peeled apples
 1 cup chopped walnuts
 1 cup raisins
 1/4 cup apple juice *or* milk
 2 cups all-purpose flour, *divided*

VANILLA GLAZE:
1-1/2 cups confectioners' sugar
 1 tablespoon butter *or* margarine
 1/4 teaspoon vanilla extract
 1/8 teaspoon salt
2-1/2 tablespoons light cream

In a large mixing bowl, combine shortening, sugar, baking soda, spices and egg. Stir in apples, nuts, raisins, juice or milk and half of the flour; mix well. Blend in the remaining flour. Drop by heaping tablespoonfuls onto greased cookie sheets. Bake at 400°

for 10-12 minutes. Combine glaze ingredients and frost cookies while warm. **Yield:** about 3 dozen.

BRAISED LAMB SHANKS

 3 tablespoons shortening *or* cooking oil
 6 lamb shanks
 1/4 cup prepared mustard
 2 tablespoons horseradish
 2 teaspoons salt
 1/2 teaspoon paprika
 1/2 teaspoon pepper
 1 cup water

In a Dutch oven, heat shortening over medium heat. Brown shanks well. Meanwhile, in a small bowl, combine remaining ingredients. Pour over the shanks; cover and cook over low heat for 2 hours or until meat is tender. If desired, skim off fat from pan juices and make gravy. **Yield:** 6 servings.

CHICKEN AND POLENTA

 1 broiler-fryer chicken (2-1/2 to 3 pounds), cut up
 2 tablespoons cooking oil
 2 ounces salt pork *or* bacon, diced
 1 garlic clove, minced
 1/2 teaspoon dried rosemary, crushed
 1 pint whipping cream
 4 cups water
 1 teaspoon salt
 1 cup cornmeal
Grated Parmesan cheese, optional

In a large ovenproof skillet or Dutch oven, brown chicken pieces, salt pork and garlic in oil. Sprinkle with the rosemary. Cover and bake at 350° for 1 hour. Remove from the oven. Transfer chicken to a warming plate. Drain excess fat from skillet; add cream and simmer until slightly thickened to make gravy. Meanwhile, for polenta, place water and salt in a saucepan. Bring to a boil. Add cornmeal, stirring constantly. Reduce heat to low; cover and cook for 15 minutes or until thick. Spoon polenta onto individual plates and top with chicken and gravy. Sprinkle Parmesan cheese on top if desired. **Yield:** 4-6 servings.

53

MEAL IN MINUTES

A menu you can make in 30 minutes or less!

Although her four children are grown and gone, Peggy Langen of Lanconia, New Hampshire hasn't put away her Meals in Minutes menus!

"This quick Chicken and Potato Saute is a family favorite I've relied on for 30 years," Peggy says. "These days, the kids still request it whenever they visit—even when we're not in a hurry for a meal!"

The pace may have slowed some at her place, but the need for speedy meals hasn't. She and her husband enjoy the many outdoor sports available in the New England area, such as swimming, skiing, biking and hiking.

"We still have a very active lifestyle, so fast meals are important. Chicken breasts are perfect. They're done quickly but taste like they've been cooking for hours."

During summer months, when fresh vegetables are abundant, Peggy serves either a zucchini and peppers saute or boiled corn on the cob. Both complement the chicken in color and flavor.

For dessert, she tops a refreshing raspberry and cantaloupe mixture with a chilled cranberry/almond sauce. (This treat can be enjoyed during winter months by substituting frozen raspberries and melon balls for fresh.)

Try Peggy's easy but elegant meal soon...and use the time you save for some outdoor activity of your own!

CHICKEN AND POTATO SAUTE

      1/4 cup butter *or* margarine
    4 to 6 boneless chicken breast
           halves
        1 medium onion, sliced
        1 garlic clove, minced
        2 tablespoons all-purpose
           flour
      1/2 teaspoon dried thyme,
           optional
    Salt and pepper to taste
        1 chicken bouillon cube
        1 cup hot water
        1 can (16 ounces) whole
           potatoes, drained
      1/4 cup red wine *or* water
    Snipped fresh parsley

In a large skillet, melt butter over medium heat. Saute chicken until browned on both sides. Add onion and garlic; cook about 5 minutes. In a small bowl, combine flour and seasonings. Dissolve bouillon in water and stir into flour mixture; pour over chicken. Cover; simmer 20 minutes. Add potatoes and wine or water; heat through. Sprinkle with parsley. **Yield:** 4-6 servings.

GARDEN MEDLEY

        2 tablespoons butter *or*
           margarine

        2 medium zucchini squash,
           cut into julienne strips
        1 sweet red pepper, cut into
           julienne strips
        1 green pepper, cut into
           julienne strips
        1 yellow pepper, cut into
           julienne strips
      1/2 teaspoon seasoned salt
    Dash pepper

In a skillet, melt butter over medium heat. Saute vegetables until crisp-tender. Season with salt and pepper. **Yield:** 4-6 servings.

CANTALOUPE AND RASPBERRY MELBA

      1/2 cup cranberry juice cocktail
        1 tablespoon sugar
        2 teaspoons cornstarch
      1/4 teaspoon almond extract
        3 cups cantaloupe cubes *or*
           balls
        1 cup raspberries
    Mint leaves, optional

In a saucepan, blend juice, sugar and cornstarch. Cook and stir over medium heat until mixture is thickened. Stir in extract. Cool. When ready to serve, combine cantaloupe and raspberries in individual bowls. Top with cranberry sauce and a mint garnish, if desired. **Yield:** 4-6 servings.

Citrus rates as a favorite of many country families! Its naturally tangy taste makes for timeless treats…morning, noon or night.

And with the recipes shown here and on the following two pages, you can count on citrus around the clock—from breakfast muffins and luncheon salads to mouth-watering main courses and delectable desserts!

CITRUS STARS! Clockwise from top: **Golden Lemon Glazed Cheesecake, Layered Fresh Fruit Salad, Orange Pork Chops, Fresh Grapefruit Cake**. All recipes on page 60.

Rise and shine…and enjoy this sunny array of citrus recipes! Sweet juicy oranges, tart lemons and other citrus fruits will tickle your taste buds in a variety of tangy recipes that add zest to meals year-round.

SUNSHINE SPECIALS. Clockwise from lower left: **Zesty Lemon Curd** (p. 60), **Mexican Carnitas** (p. 61), **Lemon/Orange Ice** (p. 61), **Orange Tea Muffins** (p. 61), **Orange Lemonade** (p. 61), **Lemon Custard in Meringue Cups** (p. 62), **Citrus-Baked Cornish Hens** (p. 61), **Orange and Red Onion Salad** (p. 61).

'My Most Memorable Meal'

$\check{C}$hildhood dinners at Aunt Carmella's house are still vivid in my mind," says Esther Perea of Van Nuys, California. "I can still smell the wonderful aromas emanating from her kitchen.

"Oftentimes, I would try to snatch a taste of something as it cooked, but Aunt Carmella would shoo me away with a wooden cooking spoon at the ready. 'Help me set the table and then we'll eat,' she'd say. Needless to say, I soon became the fastest table setter in the family!"

Esther grew up in Chicago during the 1940s and was a frequent visitor to her aunt's home.

"I always liked to watch her cook and bake," Esther says, "but she never measured anything. She would add a pinch of this, a cup or so of that. Just when I thought I had the right amounts written down, I'd catch her adding a little more of this or that!

"It wasn't until years and numerous attempts later that I was finally able to come close to her recipes! Every now and then, I have to prepare this 'memorable meal'—it takes me back in time."

The recipes featured here for minestrone, rigatoni, marinated vegetables and anise cookies are among Esther's favorites from her aunt.

PAST PERFECT. Clockwise from top right: **Meatball Minestrone, Baked Rigatoni, Marinated Vegetables, Anise Cookies.** All recipes on page 62.

CHOCOLATE DESSERT WAFFLES

Carol Ann Reed, Salisbury, Missouri

(PICTURED ON PAGE 51)

1/4 cup baking cocoa
1-1/2 cups cake flour
2 teaspoons baking powder
1/4 teaspoon salt
1/2 cup shortening
1 cup sugar
2 eggs, *separated*
1/2 cup milk
1/2 teaspoon vanilla extract
Vanilla ice cream
Chocolate sauce
Fresh raspberries

Combine cocoa, flour, baking powder and salt. Set aside. In a mixing bowl, cream shortening and sugar until fluffy. Add egg yolks. Mix well. Add dry ingredients alternately with the milk. Mix until dry ingredients are moistened. Stir in vanilla. Beat egg whites until stiff and gently fold into the batter. Preheat waffle maker and bake waffles according to manufacturer's directions. Serve waffles warm or at room temperature with ice cream, warmed chocolate sauce and fresh raspberries. **Yield:** 6-8 servings.

ZUCCHINI HARVEST SALAD

Marie Wellman, Seattle, Washington

(PICTURED ON PAGE 52)

 This tasty dish uses less sugar, salt and fat. Recipe includes *Diabetic Exchanges.*

4 cups thinly sliced zucchini
1 cup sliced celery
1/2 cup sliced fresh mushrooms
1/2 cup sliced ripe olives
1/4 cup chopped green pepper
1/4 cup chopped sweet red pepper
1 cup mild *or* medium picante sauce *or* salsa
1/2 cup vinegar
3 tablespoons olive oil
3 tablespoons sugar
1/2 teaspoon oregano
1 garlic clove, minced
Lettuce leaves

In a large mixing bowl, combine first six ingredients; toss to mix. In a small bowl or jar, combine all remaining ingredients except lettuce, and shake or mix well. Pour over vegetables. Cover and chill several hours or overnight. Serve in a large salad bowl lined with lettuce or in individual lettuce "cups". **Yield:** 8 servings. **Diabetic Exchanges:** One serving equals 1-1/2 vegetable, 1-1/2 fat; also, 113 calories, 37 mg sodium, 0 mg cholesterol, 13 gm carbohydrate, 2 gm protein, 7 gm fat.

SPEIDIS

Gertrude Skinner, Binghamton, New York

(PICTURED ON PAGE 52)

 This tasty dish uses less sugar, salt and fat. Recipe includes *Diabetic Exchanges.*

1 cup cooking oil
2/3 cup cider vinegar
2 tablespoons Worcestershire sauce
1/2 medium onion, finely chopped
1/2 teaspoon salt
1/2 teaspoon sugar
1/2 teaspoon dried basil
1/2 teaspoon dried marjoram
1/2 teaspoon dried rosemary
2-1/2 pounds boneless lean pork, beef, lamb, venison, chicken *or* turkey, cut into 1-1/2- to 2-inch cubes
Italian rolls *or* hot dog buns

In a glass or plastic bowl, combine first nine ingredients. Add meat and toss to coat. Cover and let marinate for 24 hours, stirring occasionally. When ready to cook, thread meat on metal skewers and grill over hot coals until meat reaches desired doneness, about 10-15 minutes. Remove meat from skewers and serve on long Italian rolls or hot dog buns. **Yield:** 8 servings. **Diabetic Exchanges:** One serving of beef equals 3 lean meat, 1 fat; also, 205 calories, 104 mg sodium, 42 mg cholesterol, 1 gm carbohydrate, 22 gm protein, 12 gm fat.

CHERRY BERRY PIE

Mamie Palmer, Sault Sainte Marie, Michigan

(PICTURED ON PAGE 52)

1 can (16 ounces) pitted red cherries
1 package (10 ounces) frozen red raspberries
3/4 cup sugar
3 tablespoons cornstarch
3 tablespoons butter *or* margarine
1/4 teaspoon almond extract
1/4 teaspoon red food coloring
Pastry for double-crust pie (9 inches)

Drain cherries and raspberries; reserve 1-1/4 cups juice and set fruit aside. In a saucepan, combine sugar and cornstarch; gradually stir in juice. Cook and stir over medium heat until the mixture begins to boil. Cook and stir 2 minutes longer. Remove from the heat; stir in butter, extract and food coloring. Gently fold in fruit. Cool slightly. Pour filling into pie crust and top with a lattice crust. Bake at 375° for 45 minutes or until bubbly. Cool. **Yield:** 8 servings.

PARMESAN POTATO ROUNDS

Terri Adrian, Lake City, Florida

(PICTURED ON PAGE 52)

1/3 cup butter *or* margarine, melted
1/4 cup all-purpose flour
1/4 cup grated Parmesan cheese
Salt and pepper to taste
6 medium potatoes, each sliced into 4 rounds
Italian seasoning to taste

Pour butter into a 15-1/2-in. x 10-1/2-in. x 1-in. baking pan. In a plastic bag, combine flour, cheese, salt and pepper. Shake a few potato slices at a time in the bag to coat with the flour mixture. Place potatoes in a single layer over the butter. Bake at 375° for 30 minutes. Turn slices and sprinkle with Italian seasoning. Bake for 30 minutes more or until tender. **Yield:** 6 servings.

PUT THE SQUEEZE ON: Before squeezing fresh citrus fruits for juice, roll them on a countertop, pressing down firmly with the palm of your hand. The fruits will be easier to squeeze and will produce more juice.

❖One medium orange contains 1/3 to 1/2 cup juice, and one medium lemon will yield 1/4 to 1/3 cup juice.

LAYERED FRESH FRUIT SALAD

Page Alexander, Baldwin City, Kansas

(PICTURED ON PAGE 55)

CITRUS SAUCE:
- 2/3 cup fresh orange juice
- 1/3 cup fresh lemon juice
- 1/3 cup packed brown sugar
- 1 cinnamon stick
- 1/2 teaspoon grated orange peel
- 1/2 teaspoon grated lemon peel

FRUIT SALAD:
- 2 cups cubed fresh pineapple
- 1 pint fresh strawberries, hulled and sliced
- 2 kiwifruit, peeled and sliced
- 3 medium bananas, sliced
- 2 oranges, peeled and sectioned
- 1 red grapefruit, peeled and sectioned
- 1 cup seedless red grapes

In a saucepan, bring all sauce ingredients to a boil; simmer 5 minutes. Cool. Meanwhile, in a large clear glass salad bowl, arrange fruit in layers in order listed. Remove cinnamon stick from the sauce and pour sauce over fruit. Cover and refrigerate several hours. **Yield:** 10-12 servings.

ORANGE PORK CHOPS

Elaine Fenton, Prescott, Arizona

(PICTURED ON PAGE 55)

 This tasty dish uses less sugar, salt and fat. Recipe includes *Diabetic Exchanges*.

- 6 pork loin chops (1/2 inch thick)
- 1 tablespoon cooking oil
- 3/4 cup water
- 1/2 teaspoon paprika
- 1/2 teaspoon pepper
- 1-1/4 teaspoons salt, *divided*
- 1 medium orange
- 1/2 cup sugar
- 1 tablespoon cornstarch
- 1/2 teaspoon ground cinnamon
- 12 whole cloves
- 1 cup fresh orange juice

In a large skillet, brown chops in oil on both sides. Add water, paprika, pepper and 1 teaspoon salt; bring to a boil. Reduce heat to low; cover and simmer about 35 minutes, turning once. Meanwhile, grate peel from the stem end of the orange, then cut 6 slices from the other end. Set aside. In a saucepan over medium-high, combine 1 tablespoon peel, sugar, cornstarch, cinnamon, cloves and remaining salt. Stir in juice. Cook and stir until thickened.

Add orange slices, cover and remove from the heat. To serve, top chops with sauce and orange slices. **Yield:** 6 servings. **Diabetic Exchanges:** One serving equals 2-1/2 meat, 1/2 fruit; also, 208 calories, 522 mg sodium, 50 mg cholesterol, 9 gm carbohydrate, 18 gm protein, 11 gm fat.

FRESH GRAPEFRUIT CAKE

Debbie Register, Youngstown, Florida

(PICTURED ON PAGE 55)

- 2/3 cup butter *or* margarine
- 1-3/4 cups sugar
- 2 eggs
- 3 cups cake flour
- 2-1/2 teaspoons baking powder
- 1/2 teaspoon salt
- 1/2 cup fresh grapefruit juice
- 3/4 cup milk
- 1 teaspoon grated grapefruit peel
- 1-1/2 teaspoons vanilla extract

FROSTING:
- 1-1/2 cups sugar
- 2 egg whites
- 1 tablespoon light corn syrup
- 1/8 teaspoon salt
- 1/3 cup fresh grapefruit juice
- 1 tablespoon grated grapefruit peel
- 2 teaspoons vanilla extract

In a large mixing bowl, cream butter. Gradually add sugar; beat well. Add eggs, one at a time, beating well after each addition. Sift together flour, baking powder and salt; add to creamed mixture alternately with grapefruit juice, beginning and ending with flour mixture. Gradually add milk. Stir in peel and vanilla; mix well. Pour batter into two greased and floured 9-in. round cake pans. Bake at 350° for about 30 minutes or until a toothpick inserted in the center comes out clean. Cool in pans 10 minutes; remove to a wire rack to cool completely. For frosting, combine first five ingredients in the top of a double boiler. Beat at low speed with a portable electric mixer for 30 seconds. Place over boiling water; beat constantly at high speed 7 minutes or until stiff peaks form. Remove from the heat; add grapefruit peel and vanilla; beat 1-2 minutes or until the frosting is thick enough to spread. Spread between layers and frost entire cake. **Yield:** 12-16 servings.

GOLDEN LEMON GLAZED CHEESECAKE

Betty Jacques, Hemet, California

(PICTURED ON PAGE 55)

CRUST:
- 2-1/2 cups graham cracker crumbs (30 crackers)
- 1/4 cup sugar
- 10 tablespoons butter *or* margarine, melted

FILLING:
- 3 packages (8 ounces *each*) cream cheese, softened
- 3 eggs
- 1-1/4 cups sugar
- 3 tablespoons fresh lemon juice
- 1 teaspoon vanilla extract
- 1 tablespoon grated lemon peel

GLAZE:
- 1 lemon, sliced paper-thin
- 3 cups water, *divided*
- 1 cup sugar
- 2 tablespoons plus 2 teaspoons cornstarch
- 1/3 cup fresh lemon juice

For crust, combine all ingredients and press into the bottom and 2 in. up the sides of a 9-in. springform pan. Bake at 350° for 5 minutes. Cool. In a mixing bowl, beat cream cheese at medium-high until smooth. Add eggs, one at a time, beating well after each addition. Gradually add sugar, then lemon juice and vanilla. Mix well. Fold in lemon peel; pour into crust. Bake at 350° for 40 minutes. Cool to room temperature; refrigerate until thoroughly chilled, at least 4 hours. For the glaze, remove any seeds from lemon slices. Reserve 1 slice for garnish; coarsely chop remaining slices. Place in a saucepan with 2 cups water. Bring to a boil; simmer, uncovered, for 15 minutes. Drain and discard liquid. In a saucepan combine sugar and cornstarch, stir in remaining water, lemon juice and lemon pulp. Bring to a boil, stirring constantly, and boil 3 minutes. Chill until cool, stirring occasionally. Pour over cheesecake and garnish with reserved lemon slice. Chill until ready to serve. **Yield:** 16 servings.

ZESTY LEMON CURD

Jean Gaines, Bullhead City, Arizona

(PICTURED ON PAGE 56)

- 3 eggs, beaten
- 2 cups sugar
- 1/2 pound butter, cut into tablespoon-size pieces
- 3/4 cup fresh lemon juice

Grated peel of 1 lemon

In the top of a double boiler, combine all ingredients. Cook and stir over boiling water until thickened like pudding. Remove from heat and cool. Chill until ready to serve. Spread on muffins or rolls, or serve over waffles or ice cream. Keeps well in the refrigerator up to 2 weeks. **Yield:** 3 cups.

MEXICAN CARNITAS
Patricia Collins, Imbler, Oregon

(PICTURED ON PAGE 56)

    1 boneless pork blade or shoulder roast (3 to 4 pounds), cut into 1-inch cubes
    6 large garlic cloves, minced
    1/2 cup fresh cilantro, chopped
    1 teaspoon salt
Pepper to taste
    3 large oranges, *divided*
    1 large lemon
Oil for frying
Warm flour tortillas
Shredded cheddar cheese
Salsa
Guacamole

Place meat in a medium-size roasting pan. Sprinkle with garlic and cilantro. Season with salt and pepper. Squeeze the juice from one orange and the lemon over the meat. Slice the remaining oranges and place over the meat. Cover and bake at 350° for about 2 hours or until meat is tender. With a slotted spoon, remove meat and drain well on paper towels. Heat a small amount of oil in a skillet and fry meat 1 lb. at a time until brown and crispy. Serve warm in flour tortillas garnished with cheese, salsa and guacamole. **Yield:** 12-16 servings.

ORANGE AND RED ONION SALAD
Nancy Schmidt, Gustine, California

(PICTURED ON PAGE 56)

 This tasty dish uses less sugar, salt and fat. Recipe includes *Diabetic Exchanges.*

    1 tablespoon butter *or* margarine
    1 cup sliced almonds
    2 tablespoons fresh lemon juice
    1 teaspoon Dijon mustard
    1/2 teaspoon sugar
    1/2 teaspoon salt
    1/4 teaspoon white pepper
    1/2 cup vegetable oil
    1 bunch romaine lettuce, torn

into bite-size pieces
    2 medium oranges, peeled and sectioned
    1 small red onion, thinly sliced

In a skillet, melt butter over medium heat. Saute the almonds until golden brown. Remove almonds to paper towels to drain. Combine next five ingredients. Beat in oil. Combine lettuce, orange sections, onion slices and almonds. Toss with dressing. Serve immediately. **Yield:** 6 servings. **Diabetic Exchanges:** One serving (without almonds) equals 1 vegetable, 3-1/2 fat; also, 193 calories, 207 mg sodium, 0 mg cholesterol, 8 gm carbohydrate, 1 gm protein, 18 gm fat.

LEMON/ORANGE ICE
Karen Zwieg, Lowry, Minnesota

(PICTURED ON PAGE 56)

Juice of 6 lemons
Juice of 7 oranges
    3-1/2 cups sugar
    1 pint whipping cream
    1 quart whole milk

In a large bowl, combine juices, sugar, cream and milk. Mix well. Pour mixture into an ice cream freezer and freeze according to manufacturer's directions. Serve immediately for a soft consistency or place in refrigerator/freezer. **Yield:** 2 quarts.

ORANGE TEA MUFFINS
Linda Clapp, Stow, Ohio

(PICTURED ON PAGE 57)

    2 cups sugar, *divided*
    1/2 cup fresh orange juice
    1/2 cup butter *or* margarine, softened
    3/4 cup sour cream
    2 cups all-purpose flour
    1 teaspoon baking soda
    1 teaspoon salt
    1 teaspoon grated orange peel
    1/2 cup raisins
    1/2 cup chopped nuts

Combine 1 cup sugar and the orange juice; set aside. Cream butter and remaining sugar; blend in sour cream. Combine dry ingredients and add to creamed mixture. Beat at low just until ingredients are combined. Stir in orange peel, raisins and nuts. The batter will be stiff. Spoon batter into greased 1-3/4-in. muffin cups, filling each cup completely full. Bake at 375° for about 12 minutes or until done. While still warm, dip each muffin in reserved sugar/orange juice mixture. Cool on wire rack. **Yield:** 36 small muffins.

ORANGE LEMONADE
Wendy Masters, Grand Valley, Ontario

(PICTURED ON PAGE 57)

    1-3/4 cups sugar
    2-1/2 cups water
    1-1/2 cups fresh lemon juice (about 8 lemons)
    1-1/2 cups fresh orange juice (about 5 oranges)
    2 tablespoons grated lemon peel
    2 tablespoons grated orange peel
Water

In a medium saucepan, combine sugar and water. Cook over medium heat, stirring occasionally, until sugar dissolves. Cool. Add juices and peel to cooled sugar syrup. Cover and let stand at room temperature 1 hour. Strain syrup, cover and refrigerate. To serve, fill glasses or pitcher with equal amounts of fruit syrup and water. Add ice and serve. **Yield:** 12 servings.

CITRUS-BAKED CORNISH HENS
Mary-Lynne Mason, Janesville, Wisconsin

(PICTURED ON PAGE 57)

    4 Cornish game hens
SAUCE:
    1/4 cup apricot preserves
    2 tablespoons grated onion
    1 tablespoon butter *or* margarine
    1 tablespoon Dijon mustard
    1 garlic clove, minced
Juice and grated peel of 1 lemon
Juice and grated peel of 1 orange

Remove giblets and necks from hens. Tie the legs of the hens together and turn the wing tips under the backs. In a saucepan, combine all sauce ingredients. Simmer 5 minutes. Brush the hens with the sauce and arrange, breast side up, on a rack in a large roasting pan. Bake at 350° for about 1-1/4 hours or until tender. Brush hens occasionally with sauce. **Yield:** 4-8 servings.

❖❖❖
MEATBALL MINESTRONE

1 pound ground beef
1 egg, beaten
1/2 cup chopped onion
1/4 cup dry bread crumbs
1 teaspoon salt
1/4 teaspoon pepper
1 can (15 ounces) tomato sauce
2-1/2 cups water
1 can (15-1/2 ounces) kidney
beans with liquid
1/2 teaspoon dried oregano
1/4 teaspoon dried thyme
1 cup sliced celery
1/4 cup uncooked elbow macaroni
1/4 cup chopped fresh parsley

In a mixing bowl, combine beef, egg, onion, crumbs, salt and pepper. Shape into 30 1-in. balls. In a large saucepan, brown meatballs on all sides. Drain excess fat. Add remaining ingredients except macaroni and parsley; cover and simmer 20 minutes. Add macaroni; simmer 10 minutes or until tender. Stir in parsley. **Yield:** about 2 quarts. **If Cooking for Two:** Freeze serving-size portions to enjoy later.

❖❖❖
MARINATED VEGETABLES

14 whole fresh mushrooms
Boiling water
1 eggplant, peeled and cut into
strips
1 can (13-3/4 ounces) artichoke
hearts, drained and halved
1 sweet red pepper, sliced
1 green pepper, sliced
1 sweet yellow pepper, sliced
1 jar (4 ounces) chopped

pimientos, drained
1 can (6 ounces) pitted ripe olives
or 1 cup Italian black olives
DRESSING:
1/3 cup tarragon wine vinegar
2 tablespoons olive oil
2-1/3 cups vegetable oil
2 garlic cloves, minced
1 teaspoon salt
1/2 teaspoon pepper
2 tablespoons lemon juice
1/2 teaspoon dry mustard
1/4 teaspoon paprika
1-1/2 tablespoons Italian seasoning
1/4 cup grated Parmesan cheese

In a saucepan, cook the mushrooms in boiling water for 1 minute. Drain. In a large salad bowl, combine all vegetables; set aside. Combine all dressing ingredients and pour over vegetables. Stir gently. Cover and refrigerate 8 hours or overnight. Stir occasionally. **Yield:** about 10 cups.

❖❖❖
BAKED RIGATONI

2 tablespoons cooking oil
1 medium onion, chopped
1 small green pepper, diced
1 can (28 ounces) whole
tomatoes, cut up
1 can (8 ounces) tomato sauce
1 can (6 ounces) tomato paste
3/4 cup water
1 jar (4-1/2 ounces) sliced
mushrooms, undrained
3 garlic cloves, minced
1 bay leaf
2 teaspoons sugar
1 teaspoon oregano
1-1/2 teaspoons salt
1/4 teaspoon pepper
1/4 cup chopped fresh parsley
1 pound rigatoni
2 tablespoons butter *or*
margarine
2 eggs, beaten
1 carton (15 ounces) ricotta
cheese
1/2 cup grated Parmesan cheese
Additional Parmesan cheese

In a large skillet, heat oil over medium-high. Cook onion and green pepper until tender. Add tomatoes, sauce, paste, water, mushrooms, herbs and seasonings. Simmer, uncovered, for 30 minutes. Remove bay leaf. Cook rigatoni according to package directions; drain and toss with butter. Mix eggs, ricotta and Parmesan cheese. Stir into rigatoni mixture and spoon into 13-in. x 9-in. x 2-in. baking dish. Top with tomato mixture; bake at 350° for 30-40 minutes or until heated through. Sprinkle with additional Parmesan cheese. **Yield:** 8-10 servings.

❖❖❖
ANISE COOKIES

2-1/2 cups all-purpose flour
3 teaspoons baking powder
1-1/2 teaspoons crushed anise seed
3/4 teaspoon salt
1/4 teaspoon ground cinnamon
1/4 teaspoon ground nutmeg
1/2 cup butter, softened
1 cup sugar, *divided*
1-1/4 teaspoons vanilla extract
2 eggs
1 cup blanched almonds,
toasted and finely chopped
2 teaspoons milk

Combine flour, baking powder, anise seed, salt, cinnamon and nutmeg; set aside. In a separate bowl, cream butter and 3/4 cup sugar until fluffy. Beat in vanilla and eggs. Stir in almonds and flour mixture. Line a baking pan with foil. Divide the dough in half and mold into two 12-in. x 2-in. rectangles on the foil. Smooth the surface of each rectangle; then brush with milk and sprinkle with remaining sugar. Bake at 375° for 20 minutes or until golden brown and firm to the touch. Remove from the oven and reduce heat to 300°. Lift rectangles with foil onto a wire rack; cool 15 minutes. Place rectangles on a cutting board; slice 1/2 in. thick crosswise on the diagonal. Place slices, cut side down, on baking sheets. Bake 10-12 minutes longer. Turn oven off, leaving cookies in oven to cool with door ajar. Store cookies in airtight containers. **Yield:** 3-1/2 dozen.

❖❖❖
LEMON CUSTARD IN MERINGUE CUPS
Marie Frangipane, Eugene, Oregon

(PICTURED ON PAGE 57)

3 eggs, *separated*
1/2 teaspoon vinegar
1/4 teaspoon vanilla extract
1/4 teaspoon salt, *divided*
2 cups sugar, *divided*
1/3 cup cornstarch
1-1/2 cups water
1 tablespoon grated lemon peel
6 tablespoons fresh lemon juice
2 tablespoons butter *or*
margarine
Sweetened whipped cream

In a mixing bowl, combine egg whites, vinegar, vanilla and 1/8 teaspoon salt. Beat until soft peaks form. Gradually add 1 cup sugar; continue beating until stiff peaks form. Cover baking sheet with plain brown paper. Spoon egg white mixture into eight mounds on paper. Shape into cups with a spoon. Bake at 300° for 35 minutes. Turn oven off; let shells dry in oven at least 1 hour with the door closed. Remove shells from paper. When thoroughly cooled, store in an airtight container. For custard, combine cornstarch and remaining salt and sugar. Add water and mix well. Cook and stir until thick and bubbly, about 2 minutes. Beat egg yolks; add a small amount of hot mixture. Return to saucepan. Cook and stir 2 minutes longer. Remove from the heat; blend in lemon peel, juice and butter. Chill. Just before serving, fill meringue shells with custard and top with whipped cream. **Yield:** 8 servings.

ORANGE BLUEBERRY MUFFINS
Irene Parry, Kenosha, Wisconsin

- 1 cup uncooked oatmeal
- 1 cup orange juice
- 3 cups all-purpose flour
- 4 teaspoons baking powder
- 1 teaspoon salt
- 1/2 teaspoon baking soda
- 1 cup sugar
- 1 cup vegetable oil
- 3 eggs, beaten
- 1-1/2 cups fresh *or* frozen blueberries
- 1 tablespoon grated orange peel

TOPPING:
- 1/2 cup finely chopped walnuts
- 1/3 cup sugar
- 1 teaspoon ground cinnamon

Combine the oatmeal and orange juice. Set aside. In a large mixing bowl, combine flour, baking powder, salt, soda and sugar. Make a well in the center of the dry ingredients and add oatmeal mixture, oil and eggs. Stir only until ingredients are moistened. Carefully fold in berries and orange peel. Spoon batter into greased muffin tins, filling about 3/4 full. Combine walnuts, sugar and cinnamon. Sprinkle over muffins and bake at 400° for 15 minutes or until muffins test done. Remove from tins and serve warm, if desired. **Yield:** 24 muffins.

GRILLED SALMON SANDWICHES
June Formanek, Belle Plaine, Iowa

- 1 can (8 ounces) red *or* pink salmon, well drained
- 1/3 cup finely chopped celery
- 2 tablespoons sweet pickle

relish, well drained
- 1/8 teaspoon ground pepper
- 1/4 cup mayonnaise
- 8 slices white *or* Italian bread
- 1 egg, beaten
- 2/3 cup milk

In a small bowl, combine first five ingredients. Divide and spread over 4 slices of bread. Top with remaining bread slices and dip each sandwich into combined egg and milk mixture. Brown on a well-greased griddle or skillet on both sides. Serve immediately. **Yield:** 4 sandwiches.

SHRIMP AND PASTA SUPPER
Mildred Sherrer, Bay City, Texas

- 3 tablespoons butter *or* margarine
- 1 pound fresh shrimp, peeled and deveined
- 1 cup diagonally sliced celery
- 1 jar (28 ounces) chunky spaghetti sauce

Hot pepper sauce to taste
- 12 ounces dried linguine, cooked and well drained
- 1 cup frozen peas, defrosted
- 1 tablespoon finely chopped fresh parsley
- 1 cup (4 ounces) shredded mozzarella cheese

In a large skillet, melt butter over medium heat. Saute shrimp and celery until shrimp turns pink. Stir in the spaghetti sauce and hot pepper sauce. Simmer, covered, 15 minutes. Add linguine and peas; toss well. Top with parsley and cheese. Heat until the cheese melts. Serve immediately. **Yield:** 4-6 servings.

GRANDMOTHER'S BREAD PUDDING
Sherrie Hill, St. Louis, Missouri

PUDDING:
- 1 cup sugar
- 2 eggs, beaten
- 2 cups milk
- 2 teaspoons pumpkin pie spice
- 2 teaspoons vanilla extract
- 4 cups day-old torn white *or* French bread
- 1 cup raisins

CUSTARD SAUCE:
- 3 egg yolks
- 3/4 cup sugar
- 1/4 cup cornstarch
- 3 cups milk
- 2 teaspoons vanilla extract

For pudding, combine first five ingredients in a large bowl. Add bread and raisins; mix well. Turn into a greased 9-in. x 9-in. baking pan. Bake at 350° for 50 minutes. Meanwhile, for sauce, combine yolks, sugar and cornstarch in the top of a double boiler. Gradually add milk, stirring until smooth. Cook over boiling water, stirring constantly, until the mixture thickens and coats a metal spoon. Remove from the heat and stir in vanilla. Serve pudding and sauce warm or chilled. **Yield:** 9 servings.

BROWN SUGAR OATMEAL PANCAKES
Sharon Bickett, Chester, South Carolina

- 1 egg, beaten
- 2 tablespoons vegetable oil
- 1 cup buttermilk
- 1/2 cup whole wheat flour
- 1/2 cup all-purpose flour
- 1/2 teaspoon baking soda
- 1/2 teaspoon salt
- 1/3 cup packed brown sugar
- 1/2 cup plus 2 tablespoons quick-cooking oats

In a mixing bowl, combine egg, oil and buttermilk. Combine flours, baking soda, salt and sugar; add to egg mixture. Stir in oats. Pour by 1/3 cupfuls onto a lightly greased hot griddle; turn when bubbles form on tops of pancakes. **Yield:** about 10 pancakes.

OLD-FASHIONED RHUBARB TORTE
Katherine Kalmbach, Selby, South Dakota

- 1 cup all-purpose flour, *divided*
- 5 tablespoons confectioners' sugar

Pinch salt
- 1/2 cup butter
- 2 eggs
- 1-1/2 cups sugar
- 3/4 teaspoon baking powder
- 3 cups sliced fresh *or* frozen rhubarb

Whipped cream

In a mixing bowl, combine 3/4 cup flour, confectioners' sugar and salt. Cut in butter as for pastry. Pat into a 6-in. x 10-in. baking pan. Bake crust at 375° for 10 minutes. Meanwhile, beat the eggs, sugar, remaining flour and baking powder. Fold in rhubarb and spread over baked crust. Return to the oven and bake for 35-40 minutes. Cool. Serve with a dollop of whipped cream. **Yield:** 8 servings.

ITALIAN RICE CASSEROLE

Karen Witty, Bowmanville, Ontario

1 tablespoon cooking oil
1 pound Italian sausage, sliced
1 onion, chopped
1 cup uncooked brown rice
1 sweet red pepper, sliced thin
2 carrots, diced
3 beef bouillon cubes
3 cups boiling water
1 cup frozen peas, defrosted
2 cans (4 ounces *each*) sliced
   mushrooms, drained
3 fresh tomatoes, skinned and
   diced
1/2 cup sliced green olives
3 hard-cooked eggs, sliced
1/4 cup grated Parmesan cheese

In a large skillet, heat oil over medium-high. Brown sausage. Drain excess fat. Add onion and rice. Lightly brown. Stir in red pepper, carrots, bouillon and water. Bring to a boil. Cover and simmer for 30 minutes, stirring occasionally, until the liquid is almost absorbed. Add peas, mushrooms and tomatoes. Heat 5 minutes. Remove half the mixture to a serving bowl. Top with half the olives, eggs and cheese. Layer remaining rice mixture and topping ingredients. Serve immediately. **Yield:** 6-8 servings.

BEEF/MUSHROOM POCKETS

Mary Kay Morris, Cokato, Minnesota

1 box (16 ounces) hot roll mix
1 pound ground beef
1 can (10-3/4 ounces) cream of
   mushroom soup
1 can (4 ounces) mushroom
   pieces, drained
1 small onion, chopped
1 tablespoon Worcestershire
   sauce
1 cup (4 ounces) shredded
   cheddar cheese
1 egg
2 tablespoons water

Prepare roll mix according to package directions for pizza crust. While dough rises, brown meat in a skillet. Drain excess fat. Stir in the soup, mushrooms, onion and Worcestershire sauce. Remove from heat. Divide the dough into eight pieces. Form each piece into a ball. On a lightly floured surface, roll each ball into an 8-in. circle. Place circles on two lightly greased cookie sheets. Divide meat mixture over eight circles. Top with cheese. Moisten

edges of dough and fold in half. Press edges firmly together with a fork. Prick top of dough. Beat egg and water; brush over each pocket. Bake at 400° for about 20 minutes. **Yield:** 8 servings.

OIL SPILLS: Add 1/2 teaspoon salt to oil before frying to prevent splatters. Then omit salt from the recipe.

ZESTY ZUCCHINI SKILLET

Barbara Winders, Spencer, Indiana

 This tasty dish uses less sugar, salt and fat. Recipe includes *Diabetic Exchanges*.

2 tablespoons cooking oil
4 cups diced zucchini
1 cup chopped onion
1 cup chopped carrots
1/2 green pepper, sliced thin
3/4 cup chopped celery
1/2 teaspoon garlic powder
2 teaspoons dried basil
2 teaspoons dried oregano
1/4 teaspoon salt
Pepper to taste
1/3 cup picante sauce
2 teaspoons prepared mustard
1 medium tomato, diced
1/2 cup shredded Monterey Jack
   cheese

In a skillet, heat oil over medium. Cook and stir the next six ingredients until vegetables are crisp-tender. Combine basil, oregano, salt, pepper, picante sauce and mustard; pour into skillet. Cook and stir for 3 minutes. Gently stir in tomatoes; heat through. Sprinkle with cheese and serve immediately. **Yield:** 8 side-dish servings. **Diabetic Exchanges:** One serving equals 1-1/2 vegetable, 1 fat; also, 83 calories, 162 gm sodium, 8 mg cholesterol, 6 gm carbohydrate, 3 gm protein, 6 gm fat.

GRITS CASSEROLE

Georgia Johnston, Auburndale, Florida

4 cups water
1 teaspoon salt
1 cup quick-cooking grits
4 eggs, lightly beaten
1 pound pork sausage,
   browned and drained
1-1/2 cups (6 ounces) shredded
   sharp cheddar cheese, *divided*
1/2 cup milk
1/4 cup butter *or* margarine,
   softened

In a saucepan, bring water and salt to a boil. Slowly stir in grits. Reduce heat and cook 4-5 minutes, stirring occasionally. Remove grits from heat and add a small amount of hot grits into the eggs; return to saucepan. Stir in sausage, 1 cup cheese, milk and butter; stir until the butter melts. Pour into a greased 13-in. x 9-in. x 2-in. baking pan. Sprinkle with remaining cheese. Bake at 350° for 50-55 minutes or until the top begins to brown. **Yield:** 10-12 servings.

CHILIES RELLENOS

Irene Martin, Portales, New Mexico

1 can (7 ounces) whole green
   chilies
2 cups (8 ounces) shredded
   Monterey Jack cheese
2 cups (8 ounces) shredded
   cheddar cheese
3 eggs
3 cups milk
1 cup biscuit mix
Seasoned salt to taste
Salsa

Split chilies; rinse and remove seeds. Dry on paper towels. Arrange chilies on the bottom of an 11-in. x 7-in. x 1-1/2-in. baking dish. Top with cheeses. In a bowl, beat eggs; add milk and biscuit mix. Blend well; pour over cheese. Sprinkle with salt. Bake at 325° for 50-55 minutes or until golden brown. Serve with salsa. **Yield:** 8 servings.

HONEY CRUNCH COOKIES

Germaine Stank, Pound, Wisconsin

2 cups all-purpose flour
2 teaspoons baking powder
1/2 teaspoon salt
1 cup butter *or* margarine
1 cup honey
2 eggs
1 cup shredded coconut
1 cup butterscotch chips
4 cups crisp rice cereal

Sift together first three ingredients; set aside. In a large mixing bowl, cream butter. Add honey a little at a time; mix well. Add eggs, one at a time, beating well after each addition. Mixture will appear to separate. Gradually add dry ingredients; mix until moistened. Fold in coconut, chips and cereal. Drop by teaspoonfuls onto greased cookie sheets. Bake at 350° for about 12 minutes or until golden brown. Remove cookies to cooling rack. **Yield:** about 5 dozen.

DAD'S ONION RINGS

Connie Thurman, Monroe City, Missouri

4 medium onions, sliced
  1/4 inch thick
Cold water
  3/4 cup all-purpose flour
  1 egg, beaten
  2/3 cup milk
  1 teaspoon sugar
  1/2 teaspoon salt
  1 tablespoon shortening,
    melted and cooled
Oil *or* shortening for deep-fat frying

Separate onion slices into rings; soak in water 30 minutes. Meanwhile, in a small bowl, beat flour, egg, milk, sugar, salt and shortening together. Drain onions and pat dry. With a fork, dip rings into batter. Preheat oil to 375°. Fry in 1 in. of oil or shortening, a few rings at a time, for 2-3 minutes or until golden brown. Drain on paper towels. Keep warm in a 300° oven while frying remaining rings. **Yield:** 4-6 servings.

BEEF ROULADEN

Diana Schurrer, McHenry, Illinois

 This tasty dish uses less sugar, salt and fat. Recipe includes *Diabetic Exchanges*.

1 pound thin cut round steak,
  separated into 4 pieces
Coarse-ground prepared mustard
  1/4 teaspoon dried thyme
Salt and pepper to taste
  1 medium dill pickle, quartered
    lengthwise
  3 carrots, cut into sticks, *divided*
  1 small onion, cut into wedges
  2 tablespoons all-purpose flour
  1 tablespoon cooking oil
  2 cups water
  2 beef bouillon cubes
  3 tablespoons catsup
Cooked noodles

Spread steak pieces with mustard. Sprinkle with thyme, salt and pepper. Top one edge with a piece of pickle, carrot and a wedge of onion. Roll up and secure with a toothpick. Coat each roll with flour. In a skillet, heat oil over medium-high. Brown beef on all sides. Add water, bouillon, catsup and remaining carrots. Cover and simmer 1 hour. Thicken gravy, if desired, and serve over noodles. **Yield:** 4 servings. **Diabetic Exchanges:** One serving (without added salt) equals 3 lean meat, 1 vegetable, 1/2 starch, 1/2 fat; also, 250 calories, 1012 mg sodium, 70 mg cholesterol, 12 gm carbohydrate, 26 gm protein, 10 gm fat.

ZWIEBACK ROLLS

Martha Buhler, Dalles, Oregon

✓ This tasty dish uses less sugar, salt and fat. Recipe includes *Diabetic Exchanges*.

1 package (1/4 ounce) active
  dry yeast
1 teaspoon sugar
1/2 cup warm water (110°-115°)
6 to 6-1/2 cups all-purpose
  flour, *divided*
1 tablespoon salt
3/4 cup shortening, butter *or*
  margarine, melted and cooled
2 cups scalded milk, cooled

Dissolve yeast and sugar in water; set aside. In a large mixing bowl, combine 3 cups flour, salt, shortening, milk and yeast mixture. Beat well. Add enough of the remaining flour to form a soft dough. Turn out onto a lightly floured board; knead until smooth and elastic, about 6-8 minutes. Dough should be soft. Place dough in a lightly greased bowl; cover and allow to rise in a warm place until doubled, about 1 hour. Punch dough down and divide into four pieces. Divide three of the pieces into eight pieces each; shape into smooth balls and place on greased baking sheets. Divide remaining dough into 24 balls. Press 1 small ball atop each larger ball. Cover and let rise until doubled, about 45 minutes. Bake at 375° for 30 minutes or until golden. **Yield:** 24 rolls. **Diabetic Exchanges:** One serving (prepared with shortening and skim milk) equals 2 starch, 1 fat; also, 186 calories, 299 mg sodium, 0 mg cholesterol, 27 gm carbohydrate, 4 gm protein, 6 gm fat. **If Cooking for Two:** Freeze baked rolls in heavy-duty freezer bags or freezer containers. Thaw when ready to eat.

POTATO SOUP WITH SAUSAGE

Dorothy Althause, Magalia, California

1 pound pork sausage links,
  cut into 1/4-inch slices
1 cup sliced celery
1/2 cup chopped onion
1/2 teaspoon dried thyme
1/2 teaspoon salt
2 tablespoons all-purpose flour

1 can (14-1/2 ounces) chicken
  broth
1/2 cup water
4 medium potatoes, pared and
  diced (about 4 cups)
1 cup milk
1 cup sliced green beans,
  partially cooked
Fresh chopped parsley

In a heavy skillet, brown sausage over medium heat. Remove sausage and set aside. Drain all but 1 tablespoon fat; saute celery, onion, thyme and salt. Cook until onion is tender. Stir in flour; cook 1 minute. Gradually add broth and water, stirring until the mixture comes to a boil. Add potatoes; cover and simmer 25 minutes or until potatoes are tender. Allow soup to cool. Puree 2 cups in blender or food processor; return to kettle. Add milk, beans and sausage; heat through. Garnish with parsley. **Yield:** 6 servings. **If Cooking for Two:** Freeze serving-size portions to enjoy later.

CRANBERRY CHICKEN SALAD

Gertrude Zelepuza, Aberdeen, Washington

1 package (3 ounces)
  strawberry-flavored gelatin
1 cup boiling water
1 can (16 ounces) jellied
  cranberry sauce
3 cups cubed cooked chicken
1 cup diagonally sliced celery
1 jar (2 ounces) chopped
  pimiento, drained
1 tablespoon lemon juice
1/4 teaspoon lemon rind
3/4 cup mayonnaise
Salt and pepper to taste
Lettuce leaves

Dissolve gelatin in water. In a saucepan, soften cranberry sauce over low heat. Add to gelatin mixture. Stir well. Pour into a greased 3-cup ring mold. Chill until firm, about 4 hours. In a large bowl, combine chicken, celery, pimiento, lemon juice and rind with mayonnaise. Season with salt and pepper, if desired. Chill until ready to serve. Unmold cranberry salad onto a lettuce-lined platter. Fill center with chicken salad. Serve immediately. **Yield:** 6 servings.

SPICE UP SALAD: When simmering chicken to be used in a salad, add salt, dried rosemary and onion powder to the water for extra flavor.

Quick & Easy Citrus Surprises

WHEN you're "squeezed" for time, fix up one of these fast family-pleasers. Some are tart, some sweet...but all are speedy!

TANGY CITRUS DRESSING
Kay Snead, Friona, Texas

Juice and grated peel of 1 lemon
Juice and grated peel of 1 lime
Juice and grated peel of 1 orange
1 cup sugar
1 egg, well beaten

In a small saucepan, combine all ingredients. Over medium heat, bring mixture to a boil and boil for 1 minute. Remove from the heat and cool. Serve with assorted fresh fruit. **Yield:** about 1-1/2 cups.

BROILED LIME SHRIMP
Mrs. Fayne Lutz, Taos, New Mexico

MARINADE:
6 tablespoons lime juice
2 green onions, thinly sliced
1 serrano chili, stemmed, seeded and minced, optional
2 teaspoons olive oil
1 teaspoon minced garlic
1/4 teaspoon salt

36 extra-large uncooked shrimp, peeled and deveined
Shredded lettuce or sliced cucumbers, optional
2 tablespoons minced sweet red pepper, optional

Combine all marinade ingredients. Thread shrimp on metal or wooden skewers that have been soaked in water. Place in a large glass baking dish and pour marinade over shrimp. Cover and refrigerate several hours. Preheat broiler or grill. Cook shrimp, turning once, until pink, about 2-3 minutes per side. Brush frequently with the marinade. Do not overcook. Serve shrimp hot or at room temperature over a bed of shredded lettuce or sliced cucumbers. Sprinkle with red pepper, if desired. **Yield:** 6 servings.

ORANGE COLADA
Dotty Egge, Pelican Rapids, Minnesota

1 can (6 ounces) frozen orange juice concentrate, thawed

6 ounces frozen *non-alcoholic* pina colada mix, thawed
1 cup milk
2 tablespoons lemon juice
1-1/2 cups crushed ice
Orange slices for garnish

In a blender container, combine first four ingredients. Cover and process on high for 30 seconds. Add ice and continue to blend until ice is liquefied. Serve immediately with an orange slice. **Yield:** 6 servings.

LEMON BUTTER TOPPING
Brenda Wood, Egbert, Ontario

1/2 cup butter or margarine
2-1/2 tablespoons lemon juice
2 teaspoons grated lemon peel

In a small mixing bowl, cream butter until softened. Add juice and peel. Blend until well mixed. Drop by tablespoonfuls onto waxed paper. Freeze until firm. Remove to a resealable plastic bag. Top piping hot vegetables or fish with 1-2 lemon balls just before serving. **Yield:** 8 tablespoon-size balls.

RASPBERRY/LIME PIE
Jane Zempel, Midland, Michigan

1 can (14 ounces) sweetened condensed milk
1/2 cup lime juice
1 container (8 ounces) frozen

IMMEDIATE HIT. Try tangy Raspberry/Lime Pie—it's a fun-to-make fruity dessert!

whipped topping, thawed
Few drops red food coloring, optional
1 cup fresh raspberries
1 graham cracker pie crust (9 inches), baked and cooled
Raspberries for garnish
Fresh mint for garnish

In a mixing bowl, stir together milk and lime juice. Mixture will begin to thicken. Mix in whipped topping and food coloring, if desired. Gently fold in raspberries. Spoon into pie crust. Chill. Garnish with additional raspberries and mint. **Yield:** 8 servings.

MELON BALLS WITH LIME SAUCE
Barbara Mctighe, Butler, Pennsylvania

1/2 cup water
1/2 cup sugar
Juice and grated peel of 1 lime
2 cups watermelon balls or cubes
2 cups cantaloupe balls or cubes
2 cups honeydew balls or cubes

In a small saucepan, heat water, sugar, lime juice and peel; bring to a boil. Reduce heat and simmer 5 minutes. Cool. Pour sauce over fruit and toss to coat. Chill 4 hours. **Yield:** 12-16 servings.

ORANGE BARBECUED TURKEY
Lynn Zukas, Spencer, Massachusetts

4 turkey breast steaks (about 1-1/4 pounds)
1/2 cup orange juice
1 teaspoon grated orange peel
1 tablespoon cooking oil
2 teaspoons Worcestershire sauce
1 teaspoon dry mustard
1/2 teaspoon ground pepper
1/8 teaspoon garlic powder or 1 garlic clove, minced

Place turkey in a shallow glass baking dish. Combine all remaining ingredients and pour over turkey. Cover and refrigerate, turning occasionally, 4-6 hours or overnight. Grill or broil steaks until done, about 3-5 minutes per side. Do not overcook. **Yield:** about 4 servings.

Cook up a feast for your family with this cornucopia of country recipes.

Start with steaming bowls of Wisconsin Potato Cheese Soup, garnished with crispy croutons. Next, sample the savory flavors of Osso Buco (braised veal shanks) or the zesty Southwestern Beef Brisket with tender vegetables. Top it all off with slices of Sweet Potato Pie served with dollops of whipped cream!

HEARTY HARVEST. Clockwise from top: **Sweet Potato Pie**, **Southwestern Beef Brisket**, **Wisconsin Potato Cheese Soup**, **Osso Buco**. All recipes on page 75.

S et out the soup bowls and slice the homemade bread...then sit down and help yourself to this hearty and healthful meal! It's plain and simple country cooking at its best.

SOUP'S ON! Peasant Bean Soup (p. 75), Whole Wheat French Bread (p. 76).

MEAL IN MINUTES

A menu you can make in 30 minutes or less!

Grandmothers are known for elaborate, patiently prepared meals. Occasionally, though, even a grandma needs to be quick in the kitchen!

Just ask Faye Johnson of Connersville, Indiana. "With two grown children and two grandchildren nearby, plus a variety of activities, I'm almost as busy today as I was when my family was growing up," she assures. "So I still appreciate 'Meals in Minutes'!"

A member of the ladies' auxiliary, an avid gardener, a seamstress and a Sunday school teacher, Faye enjoys full and rewarding days. Even so, she insists on cooking "from scratch" for herself and husband Clair.

"I like to experiment, adding my own little touches," she says. "I usually prepare a new recipe 'as is' just once. After that, it's never the same!"

The first time you prepare Faye's favorite fast menu, which she shares at right, you'll appreciate its simplicity and adaptability. The savory vegetable soup uses either beef or chicken leftovers to make a hearty, economical entree in no time at all.

The golden garlic bread is a speedy but zesty accompaniment that takes just minutes to brown in the broiler.

And the caramel dumplings, simmering on the back burner during dinner, will fill the kitchen with such a wonderful fragrance that you can be

sure everyone will save room for dessert!

QUICK VEGETABLE SOUP

      1 quart chicken broth *or* stock
      1 can (16 ounces) tomatoes
  1/2 cup chopped onion
  1/2 cup chopped cabbage
      1 package (10 ounces) frozen
          mixed vegetables, thawed
  1/2 teaspoon dried basil
  1/8 teaspoon pepper
Dash sugar
  1/4 cup uncooked elbow
          macaroni
      1 cup leftover cubed cooked
          chicken *or* beef roast

In a large saucepan or Dutch oven, bring broth, tomatoes, onion, cabbage, vegetables and seasonings to a boil. Add macaroni and simmer 10 minutes or until tender. Add meat and heat through. **Yield:** 6 servings.

TOASTY GARLIC BREAD

      1 French bread (12 to 15
          inches), cut into 1-inch slices
  1/2 cup butter *or* margarine,
          softened
Grated Parmesan cheese
Parsley flakes
Garlic powder

Spread both sides of bread with butter. Place, cut side down, on a cookie sheet. Sprinkle one side with cheese, parsley and garlic powder. Broil 4 in. from the heat until light golden brown. Turn slices and repeat with other side. Serve immediately. **Yield:** about 12-15 slices.

CARAMEL DUMPLINGS

      2 tablespoons butter *or*
          margarine
  1-1/2 cups packed brown sugar
  1-1/2 cups water
DUMPLINGS:
  1-1/4 cups all-purpose flour
  1/2 cup sugar
      2 teaspoons baking powder
  1/2 teaspoon salt
  1/2 cup milk
      2 tablespoons butter *or*
          margarine, softened
      2 teaspoons vanilla extract
  1/2 cup coarsely chopped
          peeled apple, optional

In a skillet, heat the unsoftened butter, brown sugar and water to boiling. Reduce heat to simmer. Meanwhile, mix together all dumpling ingredients. Drop by tablespoonfuls into the simmering sauce. Cover tightly and simmer 20 minutes. Do not lift lid. Serve warm with cream or ice cream, if desired. **Yield:** 6-8 servings.

BEST COOK

Florence Ladwig
Monroe, Wisconsin

They say the way to a man's heart is through his stomach—just ask Walter Ladwig of Monroe, Wisconsin. He has been enjoying the good cooking—and company—of his wife, Florence, for 57 years!

"She's not only an exceptional cook, she's a very special lady," Walter wrote in a touching letter. "She's always there to help out, whether it's baking for the church, school or a family event. There's always enough love—*and food*—to go around."

Florence's cooking talent and caring attitude was evident at an early age. When she was 15, her aunt died, so Florence gave up her high school education to care for her uncle and *nine* cousins!

"The two oldest boys helped me, but I had to do all the cooking, cleaning and ironing," Florence relates. "It was very rewarding, but at the same time very taxing.

"I learned a lot about cooking during the 2 years I was there. I'm very proud I kept them together."

Doughnuts Draw Crowds

One of Florence's favorite recipes —Mashed Potato Doughnuts—has become a tradition at the annual ice cream social sponsored at her church.

"Her doughnuts have great drawing power," Walter says. "People come from all over to get them. There's never enough to go around."

She taught baking at the local technical college for 12 years,

teaching adults to make bread and holiday treats. And on George Washington's birthday each year, she bakes cherry pies for the Future Farmers club to serve to the high school faculty.

Florence says there aren't any real "secrets" to her cooking. "All I do is cook and make it taste good," she explains. "I seem to have a knack for putting things together and making them turn out pretty good."

One of her specialties is Steamed Cranberry Pudding (pictured at left). "It was handed down to me by my Great-Aunt Sarah. It's really an old English dessert that I always make during the holidays."

For guaranteed good eating, give Florence's special recipes a try.

STEAMED CRANBERRY PUDDING

1/3 cup hot water
1 tablespoon baking soda
2 cups (8 ounces) cranberries, chopped
1/2 cup molasses
1 tablespoon sugar
1/4 teaspoon salt
1-1/2 cups all-purpose flour
BUTTER SAUCE:
1 cup sugar
1/2 cup butter
1/2 cup half-and-half cream

In a mixing bowl, combine water and baking soda. Immediately add all remaining pudding ingredients; mix well. Pour batter into a well-greased 1-qt. pudding mold. (If you don't have a pudding mold, use an ovenproof bowl and cover tightly with foil.) Put a rack in the bottom of a large kettle. Place pudding mold or bowl on rack. Add boiling water to 1-in. depth. Cover kettle and boil gently, replacing water as needed. Steam 1 hour or until cake tests done. Cool for 10 minutes; unmold. For sauce, heat all ingredients in a saucepan until butter is melted and sugar is dissolved. Serve pudding and sauce warm. **Yield:** 8-10 servings.

MASHED POTATO DOUGHNUTS

2 cups sugar, *divided*
1 teaspoon salt
1 teaspoon ground nutmeg
1 teaspoon vanilla extract

1/4 cup butter *or* margarine, softened
1 cup cold mashed potatoes
2 eggs, beaten
2/3 cup milk
4-1/2 cups all-purpose flour
1 tablespoon baking powder
1/2 teaspoon ground cinnamon
Shortening *or* oil for deep-fat frying

In a mixing bowl, combine 1 cup sugar, salt, nutmeg, vanilla and butter. Add potatoes; mix well. Add eggs and milk; mix well. Stir in the flour and baking powder. Chill thoroughly. On a lightly floured board, roll out half the dough to 1/2-in. thickness. Cut into 4-in. x 1-1/2-in. strips; roll in flour and tie into knots. Preheat shortening or oil to 375°; fry doughnuts until golden on both sides, turning with a slotted spoon. Drain on paper towels. Repeat until all doughnuts are fried. Combine remaining sugar and cinnamon; roll the warm doughnuts in mixture. Serve immediately. **Yield:** about 2-1/2 dozen.

SWISS AND HAM PIE

1 unbaked pie pastry (9 *or* 10 inches)
1 tablespoon butter *or* margarine
1/4 cup finely chopped onion
1 cup chopped cooked ham
1-1/2 cups (6 ounces) shredded Swiss cheese
1 tablespoon all-purpose flour
3 eggs, lightly beaten
1-1/2 cups milk
1 teaspoon dry mustard
1/8 teaspoon pepper

Bake pastry at 450° for 7 minutes or just until lightly browned. Remove from oven and reduce temperature to 325°. Melt butter in a skillet; cook onion until tender. Remove from the heat and stir in ham. Place in pie shell. In a bowl, toss together cheese and flour. Add eggs, milk, mustard and pepper; pour over ham. Bake for 35-40 minutes or until center is almost set. Let stand 10-15 minutes before cutting. **Yield:** 6 servings.

"BREAK" THE MOLD: To remove a pudding or gelatin salad from its mold, just dip the mold into warm water for a few seconds to loosen the edges. Center a plate upside down over the mold, and, holding the mold and plate together, invert them. Shake the mold gently, then carefully lift the mold off. If the pudding or salad doesn't unmold, repeat the steps.

Few foods, week in and week out, top chicken in popularity. But few items are as difficult to come by as a deliciously different chicken dish to serve a hungry family!

If that's true for you, too, your problem's a thing of the past—beginning with the four flavorful chicken treats on this page. Try each of them…there's lots of great-tasting country eating that awaits you and your family.

COUNTRY-BEST CHICKEN. Clockwise from top: **Hot Chicken Salad**, **Hungarian Chicken**, **Chickaritos**, **Crispy Chicken Wings**. All recipes on page 76.

For finger-lickin'-good flavor and freshness, chicken is the champion. And when it comes to variety, these recipes win hands-down. Feast on delicious potpies, casseroles, soups and main dishes—they're all bursting with the goodness of chicken!

PICK OF THE CHICKEN. Clockwise from lower left: **Dilled Chicken Soup** (p. 77), **Sunday Fried Chicken** (p. 77), **Frosted Chicken Salad** (p. 78), **Cheddar Chicken Potpie** (p. 77), **Greek Roasted Chicken and Potatoes** (p. 78), **Garlic-Roasted Chicken** (p. 78), **Chicken and Dumplings** (p. 77), **Chicken Cacciatore** (p. 78).

Oh, what fun it is to fill the kitchen with the irresistible aroma of holiday baking...especially when you're making the Christmas treats featured here!

Each one of these festive breads is just right for eating or wrapping up for gift-giving. Better watch out...making these pretty, palate-pleasing recipes is apt to become a regular tra-

YULETIDE TREASURES. Top to bottom: **Christmas Stollen** (p. 78), **Cranberry Christmas Canes** (p. 79), **Butter Rings** (p. 78).

WISCONSIN POTATO CHEESE SOUP

Darlene Alexander, Nekoosa, Wisconsin

(PICTURED ON PAGE 67)

2 tablespoons butter *or* margarine
1/3 cup chopped celery
1/3 cup chopped onion
4 cups diced peeled potatoes
3 cups chicken broth
2 cups milk
1-1/2 teaspoons salt
1/4 teaspoon pepper
Dash paprika
2 cups (8 ounces) shredded cheddar cheese
Croutons
Fresh chopped parsley

In a large saucepan, melt butter over medium-high heat. Saute celery and onion until tender. Add potatoes and broth. Cover and simmer until potatoes are tender, about 12 minutes. In batches, puree potato mixture in a blender or food processor. Return to saucepan. Stir in milk and seasonings. Add the cheese and heat only until melted. Garnish with croutons and parsley. **Yield:** 8 servings.

OSSO BUCO

Karen Jaffe, Short Hills, New Jersey

(PICTURED ON PAGE 67)

1/3 cup all-purpose flour
1 teaspoon salt
1/2 teaspoon pepper
4 to 6 veal shanks (2 inches thick)
5 tablespoons olive oil
1 teaspoon Italian seasoning
1/2 teaspoon sage
1 medium onion, chopped
1 garlic clove, minced
2 carrots, sliced
1 celery stalk, cut in 1/2-inch slices
1-1/2 cups dry white wine *or* chicken broth
1 can (10-3/4 ounces) condensed chicken broth
2 tablespoons tomato paste
GREMOLATA:
2 garlic cloves, minced
1-1/2 tablespoons chopped parsley
1 tablespoon grated lemon peel

Combine flour, salt and pepper; dredge meat. In a large skillet, heat the oil on high. Brown meat on all sides. Lay the shanks flat in a Dutch oven or oblong baking dish and sprinkle with Italian seasoning and sage. Combine onion, garlic, carrots and celery. Sprinkle over meat. In a small bowl, whisk together wine, broth and tomato paste. Pour over vegetables. Cover and bake at 325° for 2 hours or until fork-tender. Just before serving, combine Gremolata ingredients; sprinkle over each shank. Serve immediately. **Yield:** 4-6 servings.

SOUTHWESTERN BEEF BRISKET

Lois McAtee, Oceanside, California

(PICTURED ON PAGE 67)

1 fresh beef brisket (3 pounds)
1 teaspoon salt
1/4 teaspoon black pepper
2 tablespoons cooking oil
1-1/2 cups water
1 can (8 ounces) tomato sauce
1 small onion, chopped
2 tablespoons red wine vinegar
1 tablespoon chili powder
1 teaspoon dried oregano
3/4 teaspoon cumin
1/2 teaspoon garlic powder
1/4 teaspoon salt
1/8 to 1/4 teaspoon ground red pepper
1/8 teaspoon black pepper
3 medium sweet red peppers, cut into strips
1-1/2 cups sliced carrots (1-inch chunks)

Season beef with salt and pepper. In a Dutch oven, heat oil; brown beef on both sides. Meanwhile, combine all remaining ingredients except red peppers and carrots. Pour over meat. Cover and bake at 325° for 2 hours. Add red peppers and carrots; bake 1 hour longer or until meat is tender. Remove meat from the pan; allow to stand 15 minutes before cutting. Thicken juices with a little flour or cook over high heat to reduce and thicken. **Yield:** 10-12 servings.

SWEET POTATO PIE

Shari Millican, Smyrna, Georgia

(PICTURED ON PAGE 67)

1-1/4 cups sugar
1/2 teaspoon ground cinnamon
1/2 teaspoon ground nutmeg
2 eggs
1 can (12 ounces) evaporated milk
1 teaspoon vanilla extract
1-1/2 cups mashed cooked sweet potatoes

1 unbaked pie crust (9 inches)
TOPPING:
1/3 cup butter *or* margarine
1/3 cup all-purpose flour
1/2 cup packed brown sugar
1/2 cup shredded coconut
1/2 cup chopped pecans
Whipped topping *or* ice cream

In a mixing bowl, blend sugar and spices. Beat eggs; add milk and vanilla. Combine with sugar mixture. Stir in potatoes; beat until smooth. Pour into pie shell. Bake at 425° for 15 minutes. Reduce heat to 350° and bake for an additional 30 minutes. Combine topping ingredients. Remove pie from the oven; sprinkle with topping. Bake 10-15 minutes or until topping is golden brown. Cool on wire rack. Store in the refrigerator. Serve with whipped topping or ice cream. **Yield:** 6-8 servings.

PEASANT BEAN SOUP

Bertha McClung, Summersville, West Virginia

(PICTURED ON PAGE 68)

 This tasty dish uses less sugar, salt and fat. Recipe includes *Diabetic Exchanges*.

1 pound great northern beans, washed and sorted
2-1/2 quarts cold water, *divided*
3 carrots, sliced
3 celery stalks, sliced
2 medium onions, chopped
1 garlic clove, minced
1 can (16 ounces) stewed tomatoes, cut up
1 to 2 bay leaves
2 tablespoons olive oil
Salt and pepper to taste

Soak beans overnight in 2 qts. water. Add remaining water to softened beans and bring to a boil; reduce heat and simmer 30 minutes. Add all remaining ingredients; simmer 60 minutes or until beans are tender. Remove bay leaves before serving. **Yield:** 8 servings. **Diabetic Exchanges:** One serving equals 2 starch, 2 vegetable, 1/2 meat, 1/2 fat; also, 263 calories, 774 mg sodium, 0 mg cholesterol, 45 gm carbohydrate, 15 gm protein, 5 gm fat.

75

WHOLE WHEAT FRENCH BREAD

Roseann Loker, Colon, Michigan

(PICTURED ON PAGE 68)

    5 to 5-1/4 cups all-purpose
      flour
    2 cups stone-ground whole
      wheat flour
    2 packages (1/4 ounce *each*)
      active dry yeast
  2-1/2 cups water
    1 tablespoon sugar
    1 tablespoon salt
    1 tablespoon butter *or* margarine
Yellow cornmeal
    1 egg white, beaten
    1 tablespoon water

Combine flours. In a large mixing bowl, combine 3 cups flour mixture and the yeast. Set aside. Heat water, sugar, salt and butter to 115°-120°. Add to flour and yeast. Beat with an electric mixer on low for 30 seconds; increase speed to medium and beat 3 additional minutes. Stir in by hand enough remaining flour to make a soft dough. Knead on a lightly floured board until smooth and elastic, about 6-8 minutes. Place dough in a greased bowl; cover and allow to rise in a warm place until doubled, about 1 hour. Punch dough down; divide in half and let rest 10 minutes. Roll each half into a 15-in. x 12-in. rectangle. Roll up, jelly-roll style, starting with the long side. Pinch to seal and turn ends under to form a smooth loaf. Sprinkle two baking sheets with cornmeal and place each loaf, seam side down, on a greased baking sheet. Make slashes every 2-1/2 in. in the top of each loaf. Beat egg white and water; brush some over loaves. Cover and let rise until doubled, about 1 hour. Bake at 375° for 20 minutes. Brush again with egg white mixture and bake 20 minutes more. **Yield:** 2 loaves.

HOT CHICKEN SALAD

Michelle Wise, Spring Mills, Pennsylvania

(PICTURED ON PAGE 71)

✓ This tasty dish uses less sugar, salt and fat. Recipe includes *Diabetic Exchanges.*

  2-1/2 cups diced cooked chicken
    1 cup diced celery
    1 cup sliced fresh mushrooms
    1 tablespoon minced onion
    1 teaspoon lemon juice
  1/2 teaspoon crushed rosemary
  1/4 teaspoon pepper

    1 can (8 ounces) sliced water
      chestnuts, drained
    2 cups cooked rice
  3/4 cup light mayonnaise
    1 can (10-3/4 ounces) cream of
      chicken soup, undiluted
TOPPING:
    3 tablespoons butter *or*
      margarine
  1/2 cup cornflake crumbs
  1/2 cup slivered almonds

In a 2-1/2-qt. casserole, combine first nine ingredients. Blend mayonnaise and soup; toss with chicken mixture. Spoon into a greased 2-qt. casserole. In a skillet, melt butter and combine with the cornflakes and almonds. Top casserole with crumb mixture. Bake at 350° for 30 minutes. **Yield:** 6 servings. **Diabetic Exchanges:** One serving (without topping) equals 2 lean meat, 1-1/2 starch, 1 vegetable, 1 fat; also, 272 calories, 522 mg sodium, 40 mg cholesterol, 29 gm carbohydrate, 21 gm protein, 12 gm fat.

HUNGARIAN CHICKEN

Crystal Garza, Shamrock, Texas

(PICTURED ON PAGE 71)

    6 tablespoons all-purpose flour
Salt and pepper to taste
    1 broiler-fryer chicken
      (about 3-1/2 pounds), cut up
  1/4 cup butter *or* margarine,
      divided
    1 large onion, chopped
  2/3 cup tomato juice
    1 to 2 tablespoons Hungarian
      or regular paprika
    1 teaspoon sugar
    1 teaspoon salt
    1 bay leaf
  2/3 cup chicken broth
  2/3 cup sour cream
Parsley-buttered egg noodles

Combine flour, salt and pepper and place in a plastic bag. Shake chicken, a few pieces at a time, in flour mixture. Melt 1 tablespoon butter in a large skillet. Saute onion until tender. Remove from pan and set aside. In same skillet, melt remaining butter and brown chicken on all sides. Combine tomato juice, paprika, sugar and salt. Pour over chicken. Add bay leaf, broth and reserved onion. Cover and simmer 45-60 minutes or until chicken is tender. Remove chicken to a platter; keep warm. Reduce heat to low, remove bay leaf and stir in sour cream. Heat through 2-3 minutes. Do not boil. Pour sauce over chicken and noodles. Serve immediately. **Yield:** 4-6 servings.

CHICKARITOS

Nancy Coates, Oro Valley, Arizona

(PICTURED ON PAGE 71)

    3 cups finely chopped cooked
      chicken
    1 can (4 ounces) diced green
      chilies
  1/2 cup finely chopped green
      onions
  1-1/2 cups (6 ounces) shredded
      sharp cheddar cheese
    1 teaspoon hot pepper sauce
    1 teaspoon garlic salt
  1/4 teaspoon pepper
  1/4 teaspoon ground cumin
  1/4 teaspoon paprika
    1 box (17-1/4 ounces) frozen
      puff pastry sheets, thawed *or*
      pie pastry for double-crust
      10-inch pie
Water
Salsa
Guacamole

In a bowl, combine chicken, chilies, onions, cheese and seasonings. Mix well; chill until ready to use. Remove half of the pastry from refrigerator at a time. On a lightly floured board, roll to a 9-in. x 12-in. rectangle. Cut into nine small rectangles. Place about 2 tablespoons of filling across the center of each rectangle. Wet edges of pastry with water and roll pastry around filling. Crimp ends with a fork to seal. Repeat with remaining pastry and filling. Place, seam side down, on a lightly greased cookie sheet. Refrigerate until ready to heat. Bake at 425° for 20-25 minutes or until golden brown. Serve warm with salsa and guacamole. **Yield:** 18 appetizers or 6-8 main-dish servings.

HOW CHICKEN ADDS UP: Keep this conversion in mind—3 pounds of chicken pieces will yield 3-4 cups cubed cooked chicken to use in salads and casseroles.

CRISPY CHICKEN WINGS

Nancy Lesky, La Crosse, Wisconsin

(PICTURED ON PAGE 71)

    2 pounds chicken wings
  1/2 cup butter *or* margarine,
      melted
  1/4 teaspoon garlic powder
    2 tablespoons chopped parsley
    1 cup dry bread crumbs
  1/2 cup grated Parmesan cheese
  1/2 teaspoon salt
  1/4 teaspoon pepper

Cut chicken wings in two pieces, discarding the tips. In a small shallow bowl, combine butter and garlic powder. In another bowl, combine remaining ingredients. Dip chicken into butter mixture, then into crumb mixture. Place on greased cookie sheet; bake at 350° for 50-60 minutes or until done. **Yield:** about 20 appetizers.

❖❖❖
DILLED CHICKEN SOUP
Estelle Keefer, Allegany, New York

(PICTURED ON PAGE 72)

 This tasty dish uses less sugar, salt and fat. Recipe includes *Diabetic Exchanges.*

- 1 chicken (4 to 5 pounds), quartered
- 3 carrots, peeled
- 1 small sweet potato, peeled
- 4 celery stalks with leaves, cut up
- 1 small parsnip, peeled and sliced
- 1 large onion, peeled and quartered

Few sprigs fresh dill
Water
Salt and pepper to taste
- 8 ounces thin egg noodles, cooked and drained

Place chicken, vegetables and dill in a large kettle. Add water to cover, about 2-1/2 qts. Cover and bring to a boil over high heat. Skim foam. Add salt and pepper; simmer, covered, for 2 hours. Remove chicken and vegetables; set aside to cool. Pour the broth through a strainer. Slice carrots and dice chicken; return to broth. Discard all other vegetables and bones. Add noodles to soup and heat through. **Yield:** 10 servings. **Diabetic Exchanges:** One serving (without salt) equals 3-1/2 meat, 1 starch, 1 vegetable; also, 328 calories, 65 mg sodium, 127 mg cholesterol, 19 gm carbohydrate, 29 gm protein, 10 gm fat.

❖❖❖
CHICKEN CACCIATORE
Barbara Roberts, Courtenay, British Columbia

(PICTURED ON PAGE 72)

- 1 broiler-fryer chicken (2-1/2 to 3 pounds), cut up
- 1/4 cup all-purpose flour
- 2 tablespoons olive oil
- 2 tablespoons butter *or* margarine

Salt and pepper to taste
- 1 large onion, chopped
- 2 celery stalks, sliced diagonally

- 1 large green pepper, cut into strips
- 1/2 pound fresh mushrooms, sliced
- 1 can (28 ounces) tomatoes, cut up and juice reserved
- 1 can (8 ounces) tomato sauce
- 1 can (6 ounces) tomato paste
- 1 cup dry red wine *or* water
- 1 teaspoon dried thyme
- 1 teaspoon dried rosemary
- 1 teaspoon dried oregano
- 1 teaspoon dried basil
- 3 garlic cloves, minced
- 1 tablespoon sugar

Cooked pasta
Grated Parmesan cheese

Dust chicken with flour. In a large skillet, heat the oil and butter on medium-high; brown chicken on all sides. Season with salt and pepper while cooking. Remove chicken to platter. Add fresh vegetables to skillet; cook and stir 5 minutes. Stir in tomatoes, sauce, paste and wine or water. Add herbs, garlic and sugar. Simmer, covered, for 30 minutes. Adjust seasonings, if necessary, and return chicken to skillet. Simmer, covered, 1 hour or until chicken is tender. Serve over pasta and sprinkle with Parmesan cheese. **Yield:** 4-6 servings.

❖❖❖
CHEDDAR CHICKEN POTPIE
Sandra Cothran, Ridgeland, South Carolina

(PICTURED ON PAGE 72)

CRUST:
- 1 cup all-purpose flour
- 1/2 teaspoon salt
- 5 tablespoons chilled butter *or* margarine, cut into pieces
- 3 tablespoons cold water

FILLING:
- 1-1/2 cups chicken broth
- 2 cups peeled cubed potatoes
- 1 cup sliced carrots
- 1/2 cup sliced celery
- 1/2 cup chopped onion
- 1/4 cup all-purpose flour
- 1-1/2 cups milk
- 2 cups (8 ounces) shredded sharp cheddar cheese
- 4 cups diced cooked chicken
- 1/4 teaspoon poultry seasoning

Salt and pepper to taste

For crust, combine flour and salt in a mixing bowl. Cut butter into flour until the mixture resembles a coarse meal. Gradually add the water, mixing gently with a fork. Gather into a ball. Cover with plastic wrap and chill at least 30 minutes. For filling, heat broth to a boil in a Dutch oven or large saucepan. Add vegetables; simmer 10-15 min-

utes or until tender. Blend flour with milk; stir into broth mixture. Cook and stir over medium heat until slightly thickened and bubbly. Stir in cheese, chicken, poultry seasoning, salt and pepper. Heat until cheese melts. Spoon into a 10-in. (2-1/2- to 3-qt.) casserole. Set aside. On a lightly floured board, roll crust to fit top of casserole, trimming edges as necessary. Place in casserole over filling; seal edges. Make several slits in center of crust for steam to escape. Bake at 425° for 40 minutes or until golden. **Yield:** 6 servings.

❖❖❖
SUNDAY FRIED CHICKEN
Audrey Read, Fraser Lake, British Columbia

(PICTURED ON PAGE 72)

- 2 cups all-purpose flour
- 1/2 cup cornmeal
- 2 tablespoons salt
- 2 tablespoons dry mustard
- 2 tablespoons paprika
- 2 tablespoons garlic salt
- 1 tablespoon celery salt
- 1 tablespoon pepper
- 1 teaspoon ground ginger
- 1/2 teaspoon dried thyme
- 1/2 teaspoon dried oregano
- 1 broiler-fryer chicken (2-1/2 to 3-1/2 pounds), cut up

Cooking oil

Combine all ingredients except chicken and oil. Place about 1 cup flour mixture in a paper or plastic bag. Shake a few chicken pieces in the bag at a time, coating well. On medium-high, heat 1/4 in. of oil in a large skillet. Brown chicken on all sides; remove to a large shallow baking pan. Bake, uncovered, at 350° for 45-60 minutes or until done. Recipe makes enough coating for three chickens. Store unused mixture in an airtight container. **Yield:** 4-6 servings.

> **TIME-SAVING CHICKEN TIPS:**
> Combine your favorite dry ingredients for breading chicken and store in a plastic bag or airtight container. Next time you prepare chicken, the breading will be ready!
>
> ❖When preparing a braised chicken dish such as fricassee, save time by using a pressure cooker. Follow manufacturer's instructions for cooking chicken.

FROSTED CHICKEN SALAD
Joyce Carpenter, Darlington, Indiana

(PICTURED ON PAGE 72)

SALAD:
    2 cups diced unpeeled red
        apples
    1 tablespoon lemon juice
    4 cups diced cooked chicken
    3/4 cup salad dressing
    1/2 cup sliced seedless green
        grapes
    1/4 teaspoon salt
    1/8 teaspoon pepper
  1-1/2 cups chopped celery
FROSTING:
    1 package (8 ounces) cream
        cheese, softened
    1/4 cup salad dressing
Lettuce leaves
Sliced apples and grapes for garnish

Line a 1-1/2-qt. bowl with plastic wrap. Combine all salad ingredients and gently press into the bowl. Cover; chill several hours. Carefully unmold onto a plate lined with a bed of lettuce leaves. Combine the cream cheese and salad dressing; frost salad. Garnish with apples and grapes. Chill for several hours. **Yield:** 6 servings.

GARLIC-ROASTED CHICKEN
Michelle Bouchard
St. Jean-Baptiste, Manitoba

(PICTURED ON PAGE 73)

    6 medium chicken drumsticks
    6 medium chicken thighs
    6 medium potatoes, peeled and
        quartered
   12 extra-large unpeeled garlic
        cloves
    1/4 cup butter *or* margarine,
        melted
    1 teaspoon salt
    1/4 cup honey

In a large roasting pan, place chicken, potatoes and garlic. Pour butter over all and sprinkle with salt. Bake at 400° for 40 minutes, basting frequently with the pan juices. Heat honey; baste over chicken. Spoon pan juices over potatoes and garlic. Bake 20 minutes longer or until chicken is tender. To serve, arrange chicken, potatoes and garlic on a platter. Skim fat from pan and spoon drippings over chicken. Serve several garlic cloves per person. Each person is to cut through the skin of the garlic and spread the soft roasted pulp over chicken and potatoes. Garlic de-

velops a mild flavor when roasted. **Yield:** 6 servings.

GREEK ROASTED CHICKEN AND POTATOES
Pella Visnick, Dallas, Texas

(PICTURED ON PAGE 73)

    1 whole roasting chicken
        (about 6 pounds)
Salt and pepper to taste
    2 to 3 teaspoons dried oregano,
        divided
    4 to 6 baking potatoes, peeled
        and quartered
    1/4 cup butter *or* margarine,
        melted
    3 tablespoons fresh lemon juice
    3/4 cup chicken broth

Place chicken on a rack in a roasting pan. Sprinkle with salt and pepper and half the oregano. Arrange potatoes around the chicken; sprinkle with salt and pepper and remaining oregano. Pour butter and lemon juice over the chicken and potatoes. Add chicken broth to pan bottom. Bake at 350° for 2 to 2-1/2 hours or until chicken is browned and tender. Baste frequently with pan juices during roasting. **Yield:** about 8-10 servings.

CHICKEN AND DUMPLINGS
Patricia Collins, Imbler, Oregon

(PICTURED ON PAGE 73)

    1 broiler-fryer chicken (2-1/2 to
        3 pounds), cut up
    3 cups water
    1 cup chopped onion
    4 celery stalks, sliced
    3 carrots, sliced
    1 teaspoon celery seed
    2 teaspoons sage, *divided*
    1 teaspoon salt
    1/4 teaspoon pepper
    3 cups biscuit mix
    3/4 cup plus 2 tablespoons milk
    1 tablespoon minced fresh
        parsley

Place chicken and water in a Dutch oven. Cover and bring to a boil. Reduce heat to simmer; cook until chicken is tender, about 30-45 minutes. Remove chicken from kettle; bone and cube. Return chicken to kettle along with onion, celery, carrots, celery seed, 1 teaspoon of sage, salt and pepper. Cover and simmer for 45-60 minutes or until the vegetables are tender. For

dumplings, combine biscuit mix, milk, parsley and remaining sage to form a stiff batter. Drop by tablespoonsful into the simmering chicken mixture. Cover and simmer for 15 minutes. Serve immediately. **Yield:** 8 servings. **Diabetic Exchanges:** One serving equals 2 starch, 2 meat; also, 276 calories, 579 mg sodium, 29 mg cholesterol, 30 gm carbohydrate, 20 gm protein, 9 gm fat.

BUTTER RINGS
Florence McBride, Harvard, Illinois

(PICTURED ON PAGE 74)

    1 package (1/4 ounce) active
        dry yeast
    3 tablespoons sugar, *divided*
    1/4 cup warm milk (110°-115°)
    4 cups all-purpose flour
    1 teaspoon salt
    1/2 cup butter *or* margarine
    3 egg yolks
    1 cup light cream, heated to
        lukewarm
Chopped nuts for garnish
ICING:
    1 cup confectioners' sugar
    1 tablespoon milk
    1/4 teaspoon vanilla extract

Dissolve yeast and 2 teaspoons sugar in milk; set aside. Combine flour, salt and remaining sugar. Cut in butter as for pie crust. Beat the egg yolks into the cream; add to the flour mixture along with the yeast mixture. Blend well and form into a ball. Place dough in a greased bowl; cover and refrigerate overnight. Punch dough down; place on a lightly floured board and divide into six balls. Using hands, roll each ball into a 24-in. rope. On a greased cookie sheet, twist two ropes together, then shape into a 6- to 8-in. ring. Pinch ends together and sprinkle with nuts. Repeat with remaining two rings. Cover and allow to rise until almost doubled, about 30-45 minutes. Bake at 350° for about 25 minutes or until golden brown. Place on wire racks. Combine icing ingredients; drizzle over warm rings. **Yield:** 3 coffee cakes.

CHRISTMAS STOLLEN
Jenny Nichols, Arlington, Texas

(PICTURED ON PAGE 74)

  1-1/2 cups warm milk *or* water
        (110°-115°)
    2 packages (1/4 ounce *each*)
        active dry yeast

6-1/2 to 7-1/2 cups all-purpose flour, *divided*
1-1/2 cups butter *or* margarine
3/4 cup sugar
3 eggs
3/4 teaspoon salt
3/4 teaspoon grated lemon peel
1/2 pound raisins
1/2 pound chopped blanched almonds
1/2 cup chopped candied fruit
3 tablespoons butter, melted

LEMON GLAZE:
1-1/4 cups confectioners' sugar
1/4 cup lemon juice
1 teaspoon vanilla extract

Combine milk or water and yeast. Let stand 3-5 minutes. Add 1 cup flour; mix well. Cover and let rest in a warm place until light and foamy, about 1 hour. In a large mixing bowl, cream butter and sugar. Beat in eggs, one at a time. Add salt and lemon peel. Stir in the yeast mixture and enough remaining flour to form a soft dough. Knead until smooth and elastic, about 6-8 minutes. Place the dough in a greased bowl and cover and let rise in a warm place until doubled, about 1 hour. Punch dough down; knead in raisins, nuts and fruit. Divide into two parts; roll each into a 15-in. x 8-in. oval. Fold each in half lengthwise and place on a greased baking sheet. Brush with melted butter. Cover and allow loaves to rise until almost doubled in bulk, about 45 minutes. Bake at 350° for 30-40 minutes or until golden brown. Cool on wire racks. Combine all glaze ingredients; brush on tops of cooled loaves. **Yield:** 2 loaves.

CRANBERRY CHRISTMAS CANES
Jan Malone, Arapaho, Oklahoma

(PICTURED ON PAGE 74)

FILLING:
1-1/2 cups finely chopped fresh *or* frozen cranberries
1/2 cup sugar
1/2 cup raisins
1/3 cup chopped pecans
1/3 cup honey
1-1/2 teaspoons grated orange peel

DOUGH:
1 cup milk
1 package (1/4 ounce) active dry yeast
1/4 cup warm water (110°-115°)
4 cups all-purpose flour
1/4 cup sugar
1 teaspoon salt
1 teaspoon grated lemon peel
1 cup butter *or* margarine
2 eggs, beaten

Confectioners' sugar icing, optional

In a saucepan, combine all filling ingredients. Bring to a boil; reduce heat and cook 5 minutes. Cool to room temperature. Meanwhile, for dough, scald milk and cool to lukewarm. Dissolve yeast in water; set aside. In a large mixing bowl, combine flour, sugar, salt and lemon peel. Cut in butter until mixture resembles a coarse meal. Add milk, yeast mixture and eggs. Combine to form a soft dough. Place dough in a greased bowl. Cover tightly with plastic wrap; refrigerate for at least 2 hours. Divide dough in half. On a well-floured board, roll out each half of the dough into an 18-in. x 15-in. rectangle. Divide the filling and spread on each rectangle. Fold each rectangle into thirds, starting with the 15-in. side. The dough will now measure 15 in. x 6 in. Cut each piece into 15 short strips. Twist each strip and shape into a candy cane. Place on greased cookie sheets. Bake at 375° for 15-18 minutes or until golden brown. Cool on wire racks. Frost with a confectioners' sugar icing, if desired. **Yield:** 30 sweet rolls.

HOOSIER CHILI
Jeanne Boberg, Muncie, Indiana

 This tasty dish uses less sugar, salt and fat. Recipe includes *Diabetic Exchanges.*

2 pounds extra-lean ground beef
2 cups chopped onion
3/4 cup chopped celery
1/2 cup chopped green pepper
3 garlic cloves, minced
1 teaspoon salt, optional
1/4 teaspoon pepper
1 tablespoon brown sugar
3 tablespoons chili powder
2 cans (16 ounces *each*) stewed tomatoes
1 can (46 ounces) tomato juice
1 can (10-1/2 ounces) beef broth
1/2 cup uncooked elbow macaroni
1 can (15 ounces) kidney beans, rinsed and drained

In a large Dutch oven or soup kettle, brown beef until no longer pink. Add onion, celery, green pepper and garlic. Continue cooking until vegetables are tender. Add all remaining ingredients except last two; bring to a boil. Reduce heat; cover and simmer for 1-1/2 hours, adding macaroni for last half hour of cooking time. Stir in the beans and heat through. **Yield:** 12 servings (about 4-1/2 quarts). **Diabetic Exchanges:** One serving (without additional salt and using sodium-free tomatoes, tomato juice and broth) equals 2 meat, 1 starch, 1-1/2 vegetable; also, 255 calories, 68 mg sodium, 45 mg cholesterol, 23 gm carbohydrate, 18 gm protein, 13 gm fat.

SPICY CITRUS SALAD
Susan Seymour, Valatie, New York

 This tasty dish uses less sugar, salt and fat. Recipe includes *Diabetic Exchanges.*

1/2 teaspoon cayenne pepper
1 teaspoon paprika
1/2 teaspoon garlic powder
3 tablespoons olive oil
1 tablespoon wine vinegar
3 large seedless oranges, peeled and sectioned
1/3 cup chopped fresh parsley
18 pitted ripe olives, cut in half lengthwise
1-1/2 quarts torn mixed greens

In a bowl, whisk together first five ingredients. Stir in the oranges, parsley and olives; allow to marinate 1 hour. Toss with greens and serve immediately. **Yield:** 6 servings. **Diabetic Exchanges:** One serving equals 1 fruit, 1 fat, 1/2 vegetable; also, 112 calories, 114 mg sodium, 0 mg cholesterol, 15 gm carbohydrate, 2 gm protein, 6 gm fat.

APPETIZER CHICKEN KABOBS
Gail Ponak, Viscount, Saskatchewan

3/4 cup soy sauce
1/4 cup sugar
1 tablespoon vegetable oil
1/4 teaspoon garlic powder
1/2 teaspoon ground ginger
2 boneless skinless chicken breasts, cut into 1-inch chunks
6 to 8 green onions, cut into 1-inch lengths
8 ounces medium-size fresh mushrooms, stems removed

In a mixing bowl, combine first five ingredients. Stir in chicken and onion; allow to marinate for 30 minutes. Soak wooden skewers in water. On each skewer, thread a piece of chicken, onion, mushroom and another chicken piece. Place on a broiler rack. Broil 5 in. from the heat, turning and basting with marinade after 3 minutes. Continue broiling for another 3 minutes or until chicken is done. Serve immediately. **Yield:** 20-24 appetizers.

CHICKEN OF CHOICE: For baked chicken with a beautiful golden-brown color, generously sprinkle it with paprika before cooking.

SUNSHINE CHICKEN
Karen Gardiner, Eutaw, Alabama

 This tasty dish uses less sugar, salt and fat. Recipe includes *Diabetic Exchanges*.

2 to 3 teaspoons curry powder
1-1/4 teaspoons salt, *divided*
1/4 teaspoon pepper
6 chicken breast halves, boned and skinned
1-1/2 cups orange juice
1 cup uncooked long-grain rice
3/4 cup water
1 tablespoon brown sugar
1 teaspoon dry mustard
Chopped fresh parsley

Combine curry powder, 1/2 teaspoon salt and the pepper; rub over both sides of the chicken. In a skillet, combine orange juice, rice, water, brown sugar, mustard and remaining salt. Mix well. Top rice mixture with chicken pieces; bring to a boil. Cover and simmer 20-25 minutes. Remove from the heat and let stand, covered, until all liquid has absorbed, about 5 minutes. Sprinkle with parsley. **Yield:** 6 servings. **Diabetic Exchanges:** One serving (without salt) equals 2-1/2 lean meat, 2 starch, 1 fruit; also, 304 calories, 66 mg sodium, 73 mg cholesterol, 36 gm carbohydrate, 30 gm protein, 4 gm fat.

CHICKEN POTPIES
Sonja Blow, Groveland, California

1 package (10 ounces) frozen peas and carrots
1/4 cup butter *or* margarine
1/2 cup chopped onion
1 can (4 ounces) mushroom pieces, drained
1/3 cup all-purpose flour
1/2 teaspoon salt
1/8 teaspoon pepper
1/4 teaspoon ground sage
3/4 cup milk
3 chicken bouillon cubes, crushed
2 cups water
3 cups cubed cooked chicken *or* turkey
1 jar (2 ounces) diced pimiento, drained
1/4 cup chopped fresh parsley
Pastry for double-crust pie

Cook frozen vegetables according to package directions. Drain. In a saucepan, melt butter over medium heat; saute onion and mushrooms until tender. Stir in flour, salt, pepper and sage. Combine milk, bouillon and water.

Slowly pour into saucepan, stirring constantly. Cook and stir until mixture boils. Reduce heat and simmer 2 minutes. Stir in chicken, pimiento and parsley. Spoon into six individual casseroles. Roll and cut pastry into circles 1 in. smaller than top of casseroles. Place atop filling. Bake at 425° for 12-15 minutes or until the crust is lightly browned. **Yield:** 6 servings.

NORTHWOODS WILD RICE
Suzanne Caquelin, Minneapolis, Minnesota

1-1/2 cups uncooked wild rice, rinsed
4 cups water
1 teaspoon salt
1/4 cup butter *or* margarine
4 slices bacon, diced
1 small onion, chopped
1/2 cup celery, sliced
1/2 cup sliced fresh mushrooms
Seasoned salt to taste
1/4 teaspoon pepper
1/2 cup salted cashews

Place rice, water and salt in a heavy saucepan. Bring to a boil. Reduce heat to simmer; cook 45 minutes or until tender. Uncover and fluff with a fork. Simmer for 5 additional minutes. Drain any liquid. While rice is cooking, fry bacon until crisp. Drain on paper towels. In a skillet, melt butter and saute onion, celery and mushrooms until tender. Add rice, seasoned salt and pepper. Heat through. Just before serving, top with cashews and reserved bacon. For a make-ahead dish, place cooked rice mixture in a 2-qt. casserole; top with cashews and bacon. Refrigerate until ready to reheat. Bake at 350° for 20-30 minutes. **Yield:** 6-8 servings.

NELDA'S SAUSAGE AND RICE DRESSING
Nelda Moore, Moore, Oklahoma

1 package (6 ounces) long grain and wild rice mix
1/4 cup butter *or* margarine
1 cup chopped onion
1 cup chopped celery
1 pound mild *or* hot bulk pork sausage, cooked and crumbled
1 box (6 ounces) stuffing croutons
1 can (2 ounces) mushroom pieces and stems
2 eggs, beaten
3 cups chicken broth

1/2 cup chopped walnuts *or* pecans, toasted
1/4 teaspoon seasoned pepper
Poultry seasoning to taste

Cook rice mix according to package directions. Set aside. In a skillet, melt butter. Saute the onion and celery until tender. Combine all remaining ingredients and place in a greased 13-in. x 9-in. x 2-in. baking pan. Bake at 350° for 45 minutes. **Yield:** 8-10 servings. Dressing makes enough to stuff a 12-pound turkey.

SEAFOOD IN TOMATO SAUCE
Jeffrey MacCord, New Castle, Delaware

3 tablespoons cooking oil, *divided*
1/4 pound fresh mushrooms, sliced
1 garlic clove, minced
1 can (16 ounces) whole tomatoes, diced
1 teaspoon dried thyme
1-1/2 teaspoons dried oregano
1 teaspoon sugar
Salt and pepper to taste
1/2 pound bay scallops
1/2 pound small shrimp, peeled and deveined
1 cup cooked rice
1/2 pound cooked real *or* imitation crabmeat chunks
3/4 cup grated *or* shredded Parmesan cheese

In a large saucepan, heat 1 tablespoon oil. Saute mushrooms and garlic 3-4 minutes. Add tomatoes, herbs, sugar, salt and pepper. Cover and bring to a boil. Reduce heat to simmer; cook for 30 minutes. Uncover and cook 10 additional minutes. Meanwhile, heat remaining oil in a skillet over medium. Cook scallops and shrimp until pink, about 3-4 minutes. Divide rice over the bottoms of four individual ovenproof casseroles. Top with shrimp and scallops. Stir crabmeat into tomato mixture and spoon into the casseroles. Sprinkle each with Parmesan cheese. Broil until the cheese melts. Serve immediately. **Yield:** 4 servings.

WHITE LASAGNA
Gayle Becker, Mt. Clemens, Michigan

9 lasagna noodles
1/4 cup butter *or* margarine
1/3 cup all-purpose flour
1 tablespoon minced dried onion
1/4 teaspoon garlic powder
1/8 teaspoon pepper

2 cups chicken *or* turkey broth
1 cup milk
1 cup grated Parmesan *or* Romano cheese, *divided*
1 can (4 ounces) sliced mushrooms, drained
1 package (10 ounces) frozen cut asparagus *or* 3/4 pound fresh cut asparagus, cooked and drained
2 cups cubed cooked chicken *or* turkey
1 package (6 ounces) sliced *or* shredded mozzarella cheese
6 ounces thinly sliced cooked ham, chopped

Cook noodles according to package directions. Drain. In a large saucepan, melt butter; blend in flour, onion, garlic powder and pepper. Add broth and milk; cook and stir until bubbly and thickened. Stir in 1/2 cup Parmesan cheese. Spread 1/2 cup sauce in the bottom of a greased 13-in. x 9-in. x 2-in. baking pan. Stir mushrooms into the remaining sauce. Lay 3 noodles in the pan. Top with asparagus, chicken, mozzarella and about 1 cup sauce. Top with 3 more noodles, the cooked ham and half of the remaining sauce. Cover with remaining noodles and sauce. Sprinkle with the remaining Parmesan cheese. Bake, uncovered, at 350° for 35 minutes or until heated through. **Yield:** 8-10 servings.

TURKEY MUSHROOM SUPREME

Jeanie Beers, Montgomery, New York

1/4 cup butter *or* margarine
1 cup diced green pepper
1 cup sliced fresh mushrooms
1/3 cup all-purpose flour
1/2 teaspoon salt
1/4 teaspoon pepper
1/8 to 1/4 teaspoon curry powder
1/8 to 1/4 teaspoon dried tarragon
1/8 teaspoon coriander
1 cup chicken broth
1/2 cup milk
2 cups diced cooked turkey *or* chicken
1/2 cup frozen peas, defrosted
1 jar (4 ounces) sliced pimientos, drained
6 puff-pastry patty shells, baked

In a medium saucepan, melt butter over medium heat. Saute green pepper and mushrooms until peppers are crisp-tender. Meanwhile, mix together flour and seasonings; stir into vegetables. Cook and stir until flour is moistened. Stir in broth and milk. Cook, stirring constantly, until thickened. Add turkey and peas; heat through. Gently

stir in pimientos. Spoon into shells and serve immediately. **Yield:** 6 servings.

APPLE CIDER POUND CAKE

Joanie Elbourn, Jamestown, Rhode Island

3 cups sugar
1-1/2 cups butter *or* margarine
6 eggs
3 cups all-purpose flour
1/2 teaspoon salt
1/2 teaspoon baking powder
1 teaspoon ground cinnamon
1/2 teaspoon ground allspice
1/2 teaspoon ground nutmeg
1/4 teaspoon ground cloves
1 cup apple cider
1 teaspoon vanilla extract
ICING:
1/2 cup sugar
1/4 cup butter *or* margarine
1/4 cup buttermilk
1/2 teaspoon vanilla extract
1/4 teaspoon baking soda

In a large mixing bowl, cream sugar and butter. Add eggs, one at a time, beating well after each addition. Stir together all dry ingredients; set aside. Combine cider and vanilla. Add dry ingredients alternately with cider mixture to batter. Mix until well blended. Spoon into a greased 10-in. angel food cake pan or fluted tube pan. Bake at 325° for about 1 hour and 10 minutes or until cake tests done. Meanwhile, combine all icing ingredients in a saucepan. Bring to a boil; reduce heat and simmer 10 minutes. While cake is warm, drizzle 1/3 of the icing over cake. Serve remaining icing over individual cake servings, if desired. **Yield:** 12-16 servings.

CORNMEAL MUFFINS

Amelia Moody, Pasadena, Texas

 This tasty dish uses less sugar, salt and fat. Recipe includes *Diabetic Exchanges.*

1 cup all-purpose flour
1 cup yellow cornmeal
1/3 cup sugar
1 tablespoon baking powder
1 teaspoon salt
2 tablespoons finely chopped onion

1 cup cream-style corn
1/2 cup mayonnaise
3 tablespoons vegetable oil
1 egg

In a large mixing bowl, combine dry ingredients. Make a well in the center and add all remaining ingredients. Stir just until mixed. Spoon into 12 greased muffin tins. Bake at 400° for 20 minutes. **Yield:** 12 muffins. **Diabetic Exchanges:** One muffin (prepared with light mayonnaise and egg substitute) equals 1-1/2 starch, 1-1/2 fat; also, 189 calories, 434 mg sodium, 2 mg cholesterol, 29 gm carbohydrate, 3 gm protein, 7 gm fat.

WHOLE WHEAT ENGLISH MUFFINS

Mildred Decker, Sandy, Oregon

1 package (1/4 ounce) active dry yeast
3 tablespoons sugar, *divided*
1/4 cup warm water (110°-115°)
1 cup milk, scalded
3 tablespoons butter *or* margarine
3/4 teaspoon salt
1 cup whole wheat flour
3 cups all-purpose flour, *divided*
1 egg, beaten
Cornmeal

Dissolve yeast and 1 tablespoon sugar in water. Set aside. In a mixing bowl, combine milk, butter, salt, whole wheat flour and 1 cup all-purpose flour. Beat well with an electric mixer. Add egg and yeast mixture; beat until smooth. By hand, stir in enough remaining all-purpose flour to make a soft dough. Knead on a lightly floured surface until smooth and elastic, about 6-8 minutes. Place in a greased bowl; cover and let rise in a warm place until doubled, about 1 hour. Punch dough down. Place on floured surface. Roll to 1/2-in. thickness. Cut into 4-in. circles. Allow to rise until doubled. Lightly sprinkle an electric frying pan or griddle with cornmeal. Bake over low heat for 10 minutes until nicely browned. Turn and bake 10 minutes longer. Cool. Store in the refrigerator. To serve, split with a fork and toast. **Yield:** about 10 muffins.

MICROWAVE MAGIC: Chicken cooked in the microwave will be moist and juicy if it is covered and not overcooked. Estimate about 7 minutes per pound for a whole chicken and 5 minutes per pound if cut up.

IF TIME gets extra-tight, you can "wing it" in the kitchen—by turning to one of these fast family favorites. They're sure to satisfy your hungry brood in a hurry!

HEARTY CHICKEN BROCCOLI SOUP

Frankie Marie Gingrich, Palmyra, Pennsylvania

1/4 cup butter *or* margarine
1/2 cup chopped onion
1/2 cup chopped celery
  3 tablespoons all-purpose flour
  1 tablespoon dry mustard
1/2 teaspoon salt
1/4 teaspoon pepper
  3 cups milk
  2 teaspoons lemon juice
1-1/2 cups diced cooked chicken
  2 packages (10 ounces *each*) cut broccoli in cheese sauce, thawed and chopped
Seasoned croutons, optional

In a large saucepan, melt butter over medium heat. Saute onion and celery until crisp-tender. Stir in flour, mustard, salt and pepper. Cook until mixture is smooth and bubbly. Gradually add milk; cook and stir until mixture boils and thickens. Stir in the lemon juice, chicken and broccoli. Simmer, stirring occasionally, until heated through. Top with croutons, if desired. **Yield:** 6-8 servings.

CURRIED CHICKEN BALLS

Judy Sloter, Alpharetta, Georgia

  2 packages (3 ounces *each*) cream cheese, softened
  2 tablespoons orange marmalade
  2 teaspoons curry powder
3/4 teaspoon salt
1/4 teaspoon pepper
  3 cups finely minced cooked chicken
  3 tablespoons minced green onion
  3 tablespoons minced celery
  1 cup finely chopped almonds, toasted

In a mixing bowl, combine first five ingredients. Beat until smooth. Stir in chicken, onion and celery. Shape into 1-in. balls; roll in almonds. Cover and chill until firm (can refrigerate up to 2 days). **Yield:** about 5 dozen appetizers.

CHICKEN TETRAZZINI

Lynnette Davis, Tullahoma, Tennessee

1/2 cup butter *or* margarine
  1 can (10-3/4 ounces) cream of mushroom soup, undiluted
  1 can (10-3/4 ounces) cream of chicken soup, undiluted
  1 jar (4-1/2 ounces) sliced mushrooms, drained
  2 tablespoons chopped pimiento
  2 cups cubed cooked chicken
  4 ounces spaghetti, cooked and drained
  1 cup (8 ounces) sour cream
Grated Parmesan cheese
Paprika

In a saucepan, melt butter over low heat. Add soups and mushrooms. Stir until well blended. Remove from the heat; add pimiento, chicken, spaghetti and sour cream. Pour mixture into a greased 13-in. x 9-in. x 2-in. baking pan. Sprinkle with Parmesan cheese and paprika. Bake, uncovered, at 350° for 30-35 minutes. **Yield:** 4-6 servings.

CHICKEN ALOHA

Beth Corbin, Sarasota, Florida

  6 to 8 chicken breast halves
  1 bottle (14 ounces) catsup
  1 can (10-3/4 ounces) cream of tomato soup, undiluted
  1 green pepper, coarsely

POULTRY IN MOTION. Chicken Aloha is a welcome way to cook a quick, delicious meal!

chopped
1/4 cup packed brown sugar
1/3 cup vinegar
  1 teaspoon dry mustard
  1 can (8 ounces) pineapple chunks with juice
Cooked rice

Place chicken in a greased 13-in. x 9-in. x 2-in. baking pan. Combine all remaining ingredients except rice; pour over chicken. Bake, covered, at 375° for 1 hour. Uncover and bake 15 additional minutes. Serve with rice. **Yield:** 6-8 servings.

CORNMEAL AND HERB CHICKEN COATING

Vera A. Head, Cumming, Iowa

  1 cup dry bread crumbs
  1 cup powdered milk
  1 cup cornmeal
  1 cup all-purpose flour
  3 tablespoons salt
  1 tablespoon dried thyme
  1 tablespoon pepper
  1 teaspoon garlic salt
  1 teaspoon celery salt
  1 teaspoon onion salt
  1 teaspoon dried oregano

Combine all the ingredients. To use, place 1 cup mixture in a plastic bag; shake chicken pieces until coated. Place on a baking pan and bake at 350° for 1 hour. Store unused mixture in an airtight container. **Yield:** Recipe makes enough coating for three chickens, each 2-1/2 to 3 pounds.

HONEY-BAKED CHICKEN

Lu Montezon, Campbellsport, Wisconsin

  1 broiler-fryer chicken (3 pounds), cut up
1/3 cup butter *or* margarine, melted
1/3 cup honey
  2 tablespoons prepared mustard
  1 teaspoon salt
  1 teaspoon curry powder
Cooked rice

Place chicken, skin side up, in a 13-in. x 9-in. x 2-in. baking pan. Combine all remaining ingredients except rice; pour over chicken. Bake at 350° for 1-1/4 hours, basting with the pan juices every 15 minutes. Serve with rice. **Yield:** 4-6 servings.

This mouth-watering meal—enhanced by the mellow glow of candlelight—is perfect for guests or family on any special occasion.

Ladle up a generous serving of New England Seafood Chowder, followed by hearty Fireside Beef Stew on a bed of egg noodles with a thick chunk of Colonial Yeast Bread. And for a delicious dessert, savor a slice of California Cranberry Torte.

CANDLELIGHT DINNER. Clockwise from right: **Fireside Beef Stew, New England Seafood Chowder, Colonial Yeast Bread, California Cranberry Torte.** All recipes on page 91.

MEAL
IN
MINUTES

A menu you can make in 30 minutes or less!

When unexpected guests come for dinner, country cooks count on quick meals. But when those guests are hungry teenagers, the fare had better be fast and filling!

Janet Roehring of Marble Falls, Texas shares just that sort of specialty this time. "I came up with this menu when one of our sons arrived home unannounced from college with a couple of friends," she relates. "I offered them a home-cooked meal, and they jumped at the idea.

"I sorted through some tried-and-true recipes and combined them in short order. Happily, the entire concoction was a success... it's still known in our family as 'the meal'!"

It's still getting a workout at the Roehring home, too, with Janet's three other college-age youngsters and their pals regularly dropping in at mealtime. "But that's okay with us," she assures. "It's always 'open house' here for our children and their friends."

You'll appreciate Janet's quick, hearty pasta and sausage bake anytime. The accompanying bean salad is a snap to put together. As for dessert, a prepared pie crust and frozen strawberries assure you'll be serving the entire meal in under 30 minutes.

You don't have to wait for unexpected guests either...enjoy this tasty, timely meal tonight!

PASTA AND SAUSAGE BAKE

- **1 pound Italian sausage, cut into 1/4-inch slices**
- **1 jar (15 ounces) spaghetti sauce**
- **8 ounces mostaccioli, cooked and drained**
- **1/3 cup grated Parmesan cheese**
- **1 package (4 ounces) shredded mozzarella cheese**

In a skillet, brown sausage. Drain. In a greased 2-qt. baking dish, combine sausage, sauce, mostaccioli and Parmesan cheese. Top with mozzarella cheese. Bake at 350° for 15-20 minutes or until heated through. **Yield:** 4-6 servings.

SPEEDY BEAN SALAD

- **3/4 cup sugar**
- **2/3 cup vinegar**
- **1/3 cup vegetable oil**
- **1 teaspoon salt**
- **Dash pepper**
- **1 can (15 ounces) garbanzo beans, rinsed and drained**
- **1 can (15-1/2 ounces) kidney beans, rinsed and drained**
- **1 can (15 ounces) great northern beans, rinsed and**
  drained
- **1/2 medium onion, chopped**
- **1/2 cup chopped green pepper**

In a bowl, combine sugar, vinegar, oil, salt and pepper. Stir in all remaining ingredients. Let marinate until serving time. **Yield:** 6 servings.

SPARKLING STRAWBERRY PIE

- **2 packages (3 ounces *each*) regular *or* sugar-free raspberry *or* strawberry-flavored gelatin**
- **2 cups boiling water**
- **3 to 4 cups frozen whole strawberries**
- **1 prepared pie crust (8 *or* 9 inches)**
- **Whipped topping**

In a mixing bowl, dissolve gelatin in water. Add frozen berries and allow to set a few minutes to thicken. When partially set, spoon into pie shell. Refrigerate. Garnish with whipped topping. **Yield:** 6 servings.

EASY AS PIE. When making pie crust, mix the flour, salt and shortening ahead and store in refrigerator until ready to use. Then just add water to make dough.

COUNTRY INN

Durlacher Hof

Box 1125, 7055 Nesters Rd.
Whistler, British Columbia
Canada V0N 1B0

Phone: 1-604/733-2963

Directions: From Vancouver, follow Hwy. 99 north to Whistler. Continue 3/4 mile past Whistler Village, left on Nesters Road to inn.

Innkeepers: Erika and Peter Durlacher

Schedule: Open year-round.

Accommodations and Rates: Seven guest rooms with private baths, $79 to $149 (Canadian dollars); includes breakfast. Ski packages available. Dinner offered several nights a week. No smoking or pets allowed. German also spoken. Handicapped accessible.

*W*ilkommen translates to far more than a simple "welcome" at Durlacher Hof in scenic Whistler, British Columbia. It also reflects the warm hospitality and wonderful food served at the charming chalet.

Several nights a week, hosts Erika and Peter Durlacher serve a hearty, home-style Austrian dinner, such as savory cream of carrot soup with crusty sourdough bread and tender pork Wiener schnitzel. But true to the name of a bed-and-breakfast establishment, Durlacher Hof's specialty is a mouth-watering multi-course breakfast.

Sample for yourself the buffet of baked scrambled eggs, crunchy coffee kuchen and blueberry scones. Then fuel up for the day with the popular "main course" of *Kaiserschmarren*, a sweet raisin skillet-baked pancake.

KAISERSCHMARREN

2 cups all-purpose flour
1 cup milk
Pinch salt
4 eggs, *separated*
1/4 cup unsalted butter, melted
1/4 cup sugar
1/2 cup butter

1/2 cup raisins
2 tablespoons confectioners' sugar
Stewed plums *or* other fruit

Mix flour and milk to a thick paste. Add salt. Stir in 4 egg yolks and unsalted butter. Beat egg whites with 1/4 cup sugar until stiff and fold into batter. Melt 1/2 cup butter in an 11-in. x 7-in. glass baking dish or a 12-in. round cast-iron pan. Pour in batter. Scatter raisins over top. Bake at 375° for about 20 minutes. Using two forks, tear pancake into pieces and allow to steam for a moment. Dust with confectioners' sugar and serve with plums or other fruit. **Yield:** 4-6 servings.

BLUEBERRY SCONES

1 cup whole wheat flour
1 cup all-purpose flour
1 tablespoon baking powder
1/4 cup sugar
1/3 cup butter *or* margarine
3/4 cup light cream
1 egg yolk
1 cup fresh blueberries
Additional sugar

In a mixing bowl, combine flours, baking powder and sugar. Cut in butter until mixture resembles fine crumbs. Beat cream and egg yolk together; add to dry ingredients. Stir with a fork just until dry ingredients are moistened. Gently fold in blueberries. Turn out onto a floured surface and knead gently about six times to form a ball. Pat dough into a circle about 3/4 in. thick. Carefully place on a greased baking sheet. Use a sharp knife to mark eight wedges, being careful not to cut all the way through. Sprinkle with sugar. Bake at 425° for 20 minutes or until browned. Break into wedges and serve hot with butter. **Yield:** 8 scones.

CRUNCHY COFFEE KUCHEN

1 cup all-purpose flour
1 cup packed brown sugar
1-1/2 teaspoons baking powder
1/2 teaspoon ground cinnamon
1/4 teaspoon salt
1/2 cup butter
1 cup bran flakes
1/2 cup raisins
1 teaspoon instant coffee granules
2/3 cup milk
1 egg
1/4 cup chopped pecans *or* walnuts

Combine first five ingredients. Cut in butter until mixture is crumbly. Add bran flakes and raisins. Set aside 1/3 cup crumb mixture for topping. Beat together coffee, milk and egg; add to remaining flour mixture. Pour batter into a greased and floured 9-in. pie plate. Sprinkle with reserved crumb mixture, then nuts. Bake at 350° for 35-45 minutes or until toothpick inserted into center comes out clean. **Yield:** 6-8 servings.

BAKED SCRAMBLED EGGS

22 eggs, lightly beaten
3/4 cup butter, melted
1/2 pound grated Parmesan cheese
2-1/2 cups hot milk
3/4 teaspoon salt
Pepper to taste

Stir together all ingredients. Place in a greased ovenproof baking pan. Bake at 325° for 35 minutes or until set. **Yield:** 16 servings.

APPLE PANCAKE

6 tablespoons butter *or* margarine, *divided*
4 medium apples, peeled, cored and sliced
6 tablespoons sugar
1/4 teaspoon ground cinnamon
1/8 teaspoon ground nutmeg
2 eggs, beaten
1/2 cup milk
1/4 teaspoon salt
1/2 cup all-purpose flour
2 tablespoons confectioners' sugar

In a skillet, melt 5 tablespoons butter. Add apple slices; cook over medium heat for 5 minutes. Mix sugar, cinnamon and nutmeg; sprinkle over apples. Cover and continue cooking on low for 10 minutes, turning apples once or twice. Set aside. Combine eggs, milk and salt; beat well. Add flour and beat until batter is smooth. Melt remaining butter in a 10-in. round ovenproof frying pan or deep skillet. Pour in batter. Bake at 450° for 15 minutes, pricking batter with fork when it puffs in center. Reduce heat to 350° and bake 10 minutes longer, pricking if necessary. Spoon apple mixture on pancake; fold over and dust with confectioners' sugar. Cut into wedges and serve immediately. **Yield:** 4 servings.

Ĕveryone loves dessert—and who could resist one of the deluxe recipes pictured here?

You'll want to dig into these delightful treats again and again…they're sweetly suited to serve at church potlucks, reunions, parties, the end of a meal…wherever dessert lovers are gathered!

DELECTABLE DESSERTS. Clockwise from lower left: **Saucy Mocha Pudding** (p. 92), **Chewy Date Pinwheels** (p. 92), **Fudge Brownies** (p. 92), **Sour Cream Pound Cake** (p. 92), **Steamed Holiday Pudding** (p. 92), **Old-Fashioned Rice Custard** (p. 93), **Strawberry Shortcake** (p. 93), **Date Nut Torte** (p. 92).

atisfy your sweet tooth (and your family's) with a cozy confection that's guaranteed to please!

These recipes use simple ingredients to make sensational desserts that are destined to become regular favorites. So you and your family can enjoy luscious, lip-smacking desserts whenever you like!

MMM-MEMORIES! Clockwise from left: **Strawberry Cream Puffs** (p. 93), **Butter Pecan Ice Cream** (p. 93), **Grandma's Chocolate Meringue Pie** (p. 93), **Family Cheesecake Squares** (p. 94).

Quick & Easy Old-Time Desserts

FOR old-fashioned taste with newfangled haste, try these delicious dessert recipes. They'll satisfy your sweet tooth speedily!

SPEEDY APPLE CRISP

Lucy Euvrard, Okena, Ohio

5 to 6 cups peeled sliced cooking apples
1/3 cup butter *or* margarine
1/2 cup all-purpose flour
1/2 cup rolled oats
3/4 cup packed brown sugar
1/2 to 1 teaspoon cinnamon

Spread apples in a 9-in. x 9-in. baking pan. Cut butter into remaining ingredients until the mixture resembles coarse crumbs. Sprinkle over apples. Bake at 375° for 30-35 minutes or until apples are tender and topping is golden. Serve warm. **Yield:** 6-8 servings.

Microwave Directions: Assemble as above using a glass baking pan. Microwave on high, uncovered, 7-10 minutes or until apples are tender. Turn pan 1/4 turn after 4 minutes. Let stand 10 minutes before serving.

BLUEBERRY AND PEACH COBBLER

Laura Jansen, Battle Creek, Michigan

2 tablespoons sugar
2 tablespoons brown sugar
1 tablespoon cornstarch
1/2 cup water
1 tablespoon lemon juice
2 cups peeled sliced fresh peaches
1 cup blueberries
TOPPING:
1 cup all-purpose flour
1/4 cup sugar
1-1/2 teaspoons baking powder
1/2 teaspoon salt
1/2 cup milk
1/4 cup butter *or* margarine, softened

In a saucepan, combine first five ingredients. Bring to a boil, stirring until thick. Add fruit and pour into a 2-qt. baking dish. For topping, combine flour, sugar, baking powder and salt in a mixing bowl. Stir in milk and butter. Spread over fruit mixture and bake at 375° for 50 minutes or until topping is golden brown and tests done. Serve warm. **Yield:** about 6 servings.

FREEZE-AHEAD PEACH PIE FILLING

Mary Ellen Thomas, Greer, South Carolina

4 quarts peeled sliced fresh peaches
3-1/2 cups sugar
3/4 cup quick-cooking tapioca
3/4 teaspoon salt
1/4 teaspoon lemon juice

In a large mixing bowl, combine all ingredients. Let stand for 15 minutes. Line four 9-in. pie pans with foil. Add fruit mixture and level; place in freezer until frozen solid. When frozen, close foil, sealing well to prevent freezer burn. Remove from pans and stack in freezer until ready to use. To bake, remove frozen peaches from the foil and place in an unbaked pie shell. Cover with top crust and seal. Brush with melted butter and cover crust edges with foil. Bake at 400° for 50 minutes. Remove foil and continue to bake about 20 minutes or until bubbly and golden brown.

FLOURLESS PEANUT BUTTER COOKIES

Maggie Schimmel, Wauwatosa, Wisconsin

1 egg, beaten
1 cup sugar
1 cup creamy peanut butter

In a large bowl, mix all ingredients. Scoop level tablespoonfuls and roll into

FAST FAVORITE. Flourless Peanut Butter Cookies don't ever stick around for very long!

balls. Place on ungreased cookie sheet and flatten with a fork. Bake at 350° for about 18 minutes. Remove to a wire rack to cool. **Yield:** 2 dozen.

> **CLEVER IDEA:** Hollowed-out orange or grapefruit halves make ideal "bowls" for relishes, fruit salads and summer desserts.

GRAMMY GILMAN'S RAISIN PIE

Ruth Bolduc, Conway, New Hampshire

1 cup sugar
3 tablespoons all-purpose flour
1 cup raisins
1 tablespoon butter *or* margarine
1 tablespoon vinegar
1-1/2 cups cold water
Pastry for 8-inch double-crust pie

In a saucepan, combine sugar and flour. Add all remaining ingredients except crust; cook over medium heat, stirring constantly, until thickened. Pour into a prepared shell. Cut several slits in top crust and position over filling. Seal. Bake at 400° for about 45 minutes or until golden. **Yield:** 6 servings.

GRANDMA BUELAH'S APPLE DUMPLINGS

Jenny Hughson, Mitchell, Nebraska

Pastry for double-crust pie
6 small cooking apples, peeled and cored
1/3 cup sugar
2 tablespoons half-and-half cream
3/4 cup maple *or* maple-flavored syrup, warmed

On a floured surface, roll out pastry to an 18-in. x 12-in. rectangle. Cut into six 6-in. squares. Place an apple on each square. Combine sugar and cream and spoon into apple center. Moisten edges of pastry; fold up the corners to center and pinch to seal. Place on an ungreased 13-in. x 9-in. x 2-in. baking pan. Bake at 450° for 15 minutes. Reduce heat to 350° and continue baking until done, about 30 minutes. Baste dumplings with syrup twice during last 30 minutes. Serve warm. **Yield:** 6 servings.

'My Most Memorable Meal'

My parents emigrated from the Ukraine to Montreal when I was a little girl," relates Lydia Robotewskyj of Franklin, Wisconsin, "and my mother brought along many of her favorite recipes to her new home.

"Mom didn't believe in going out for dinner. 'Why spend money on a meal when I can make one from scratch?' she'd always say. And she was probably right about that—her home-cooked meals were better than any you'd get in a restaurant."

Lydia learned to cook—almost without realizing it—just by watching her mother. She says Ukrainian recipes frequently call for garlic, bay leaves and various other spices.

"Meats are often coated with different kinds of glazes," Lydia explains. "That unusual blend of sweets and spices

is what gives these Ukrainian meals their unique taste and aroma."

This "memorable meal" is one of the favorites Lydia remembers from her childhood. She prepares it for special family occasions and for guests. "Afterward, people almost always ask me for the recipes," she says.

The recipes featured here for potato pancakes, cucumber salad, noodle pudding and pork roast are part of Lydia's treasured "inheritance"—each time she prepares this meal, it brings back fond memories of her mother in the kitchen.

FOND FEAST. Clockwise from bottom right: **Country Potato Pancakes, Spiced Apple Pork Roast, Sour Cream Cucumber Salad, Babka.** All recipes on page 94.

NEW ENGLAND SEAFOOD CHOWDER
Jane Chartrand, Orleans, Vermont

(PICTURED ON PAGE 83)

1 pound whitefish, skin and
bones removed
1 cup diced celery
1 large onion, chopped
5 medium potatoes, peeled and
cubed
3 tablespoons all-purpose flour
1/3 cup cold water
2 cans (6-1/2 ounces *each*)
minced clams, liquid reserved
1 can (4 ounces) tiny shrimp,
drained
1 can (6 ounces) crabmeat,
drained
2 teaspoons salt
1/2 teaspoon pepper
2 tablespoons butter *or*
margarine
1 can (12 ounces) evaporated
milk
1/2 jar (1 ounce) pimiento, drained
Fresh chopped parsley

In a large Dutch oven, place fish and
enough water to cover. Cook over medium heat until fish flakes with a fork,
about 10 minutes. With a slotted
spoon, remove fish and break into bite-
size pieces; set aside. Measure cooking liquid and add enough additional
water to equal 4 cups. In the liquid,
cook celery, onion and potatoes until
tender. Combine the flour and water to
make a paste; stir into chowder. Cook
and stir until mixture boils. Add reserved fish, clams with liquid, shrimp,
crabmeat, salt, pepper, butter, milk
and pimiento. Heat through, stirring
occasionally. Garnish with parsley.
Yield: 3-1/2 quarts.

CALIFORNIA CRANBERRY TORTE
Pat Parsons, Bakersfield, California

(PICTURED ON PAGE 83)

6 egg whites
Pinch salt
1/4 teaspoon cream of tartar
1-1/2 cups sugar
1 teaspoon vanilla extract
1 can (16 ounces) jellied
cranberry sauce
2 tablespoons raspberry-
flavored gelatin powder
1-1/2 cups whipping cream
2 tablespoons confectioners'
sugar

**Fresh cranberries *or* raspberries for
garnish, optional**

In a mixing bowl, beat egg whites until
foamy. Add salt and cream of tartar;
beat until soft peaks form. Gradually
add sugar, 2 tablespoons at a time,
and continue beating until stiff and
glossy. Add vanilla. Place plain brown
paper or parchment on cookie sheets.
Draw three 8-in. circles on the paper.
Spoon the meringue into the circles,
spreading with a knife. Bake at 250°
for 1 hour. Meringues should sound
hollow when tapped. Turn heat off and
allow meringues to stay in oven with
the door open until cool. Meanwhile,
melt cranberry sauce in a saucepan
over medium heat. Add gelatin and stir
to dissolve. Cool. Whip cream with the
confectioners' sugar; fold 1 cup into
cranberry mixture. To assemble, place
1 tablespoon whipped cream in the
center of serving platter to hold meringue in place. Top with a meringue
shell; spread 1/3 of the cranberry mixture on top. Repeat with remaining meringues and cranberry mixture. Frost
sides of torte with reserved whipped
cream. If desired, a pastry tube can be
used to decorate edges of torte. Chill 6
hours or overnight. Garnish with fresh
cranberries or raspberries, if desired.
Yield: 12-16 servings.

FIRESIDE BEEF STEW
Donna Nevil, New Glarus, Wisconsin

(PICTURED ON PAGE 83)

 **This tasty dish uses less sugar, salt and
fat. Recipe includes *Diabetic Exchanges*.**

2 pounds lean beef chuck *or*
round steak, cut into
1-1/2-inch pieces
1 tablespoon browning sauce
1/4 cup dry cream of rice cereal
4 carrots, cut into 1-1/2-inch
chunks
2 cups thinly sliced onion
1 garlic clove, minced
1/2 to 1 teaspoon dried marjoram,
crushed
1/2 to 1 teaspoon dried thyme,
crushed
1 teaspoon salt
1/4 teaspoon pepper
1 cup dry red wine *or* beef broth
1 jar (4.5 ounces) button
mushrooms, undrained
Cooked noodles

In a medium Dutch oven or 3-qt. casserole, toss meat with browning sauce.
Mix in cereal. Add all remaining ingredients except noodles. Cover and bake
at 325° for 2 to 2-1/2 hours or until the
meat and vegetables are tender. Serve

with noodles. **Yield:** 8 servings. **Diabetic Exchanges:** One serving (prepared with beef broth and no added
salt) equals 2 lean meat, 1-1/2 vegetable, 1/2 starch; also, 199 calories, 50
mg sodium, 72 mg cholesterol, 12 gm
carbohydrate, 21 gm protein, 6 gm fat.

COLONIAL YEAST BREAD
Stella Quade, Carthage, Missouri

(PICTURED ON PAGE 83)

1/2 cup cornmeal
1/2 cup packed brown sugar *or*
1/3 cup honey
1 tablespoon salt
2 cups boiling water
1/2 cup vegetable oil
2 packages (1/4 ounce *each*)
active dry yeast
1/2 cup warm water (110°-115°)
3/4 cup whole wheat flour
1/2 cup rye flour
4-1/2 to 5-1/2 cups all-purpose flour

In a mixing bowl, combine cornmeal,
sugar or honey, salt, boiling water and
oil. Let cool to lukewarm. Meanwhile,
dissolve yeast in warm water and let
stand 5 minutes. Stir into cornmeal
mixture. Add whole wheat flour, rye
flour and enough all-purpose flour to
form a stiff dough. Turn out onto a
floured board; knead until smooth and
elastic, about 6-8 minutes. Place in a
greased bowl; cover and let rise in a
warm place until doubled, about 1-1/2
hours. Punch dough down. Divide into
two balls. Cover and let rest 10 minutes. Shape into two loaves and place
in two greased 8-in. x 4-in. x 2-in.
bread pans. Cover and let rise until
doubled, about 1-1/2 hours. Bake at
375° for 35-40 minutes. Cover loosely
with foil if top browns too quickly. Remove from pans and let cool on a wire
rack. **Yield:** 2 loaves.

COOKIE CUSHION: If you're sending
cookies out of town, wrap them
individually or place them in a plastic
bag, then bed them down in a box
filled with popped popcorn. Fill all
remaining space in the box with the
popcorn, until it touches the lid.

SAUCY MOCHA PUDDING

Kathy Koch, Smoky Lake, Alberta

(PICTURED ON PAGE 86)

SAUCE:
- 1/4 cup baking cocoa
- 1/2 cup sugar
- 1/2 cup packed brown sugar
- 1-1/2 cups hot strong coffee

CAKE:
- 1/3 cup butter *or* margarine
- 2/3 cup sugar
- 1 egg
- 1/2 teaspoon vanilla extract
- 1 cup all-purpose flour
- 1-1/2 teaspoons baking powder
- 1/4 teaspoon salt
- 1/3 cup milk

Ice cream *or* whipped cream, optional

In a saucepan, combine all sauce ingredients and keep warm. Meanwhile, in a large mixing bowl, beat butter, sugar, egg and vanilla until light and fluffy. Combine flour, baking powder and salt; add alternately with milk to the egg mixture. Spread into a greased 8-in. x 8-in. baking pan. Pour sauce over the batter. *Do not stir.* Bake at 350° for 45-50 minutes or until the cake tests done. When finished, the cake will float in the hot mocha sauce. Serve warm with ice cream or whipped cream, if desired. **Yield:** about 9 servings.

CHEWY DATE PINWHEELS

Naomi Cross, Goshen, Indiana

(PICTURED ON PAGE 86)

FILLING:
- 1-1/2 cups chopped dates
- 1 cup sugar
- 1 cup water
- 1/2 cup chopped pecans

COOKIE:
- 1 cup butter *or* margarine
- 2 cups packed brown sugar
- 1/2 cup sugar
- 3 eggs
- 4-1/2 cups all-purpose flour
- 1 teaspoon salt
- 1 teaspoon baking soda
- 1 teaspoon cinnamon

In a saucepan, combine dates, sugar and water. Cook over medium heat, stirring constantly, until thick, about 8 minutes. Add nuts; cool. Meanwhile, cream butter and sugars. Add eggs, one at a time, beating well after each addition. Combine flour, salt, soda and cinnamon. Add gradually to butter mixture. Divide dough and roll on a lightly floured surface to a rectangle 1/4 in.

thick. Spread with half the date filling and roll up jelly-roll style. Wrap with plastic wrap. Repeat with remaining dough and filling. Chill dough rolls overnight. Before baking, cut dough into 1/2-in. slices. Place on greased cookie sheets 2 in. apart. Bake at 375° for about 12 minutes. Cool on wire racks. **Yield:** about 4 dozen.

DATE NUT TORTE

June Hovland, Rochester, Minnesota

(PICTURED ON PAGE 86)

- 2 eggs
- 1/2 cup sugar
- 1/2 cup packed brown sugar
- 2/3 cup all-purpose flour
- 1 teaspoon baking powder
- 1/4 teaspoon salt
- 1 cup chopped walnuts
- 1 cup chopped dates

Whipped cream

In a mixing bowl, beat eggs. Gradually add sugars and beat until well mixed. Add combined dry ingredients; mix until moistened. Stir in nuts and dates. Pour into a greased 8-in. x 8-in. baking pan. Bake at 350° for 30 minutes. Torte top will be crusty and the inside chewy. Cut into squares and serve with a dollop of whipped cream. **Yield:** 9 servings.

STEAMED HOLIDAY PUDDING

Bernadean Bichel, Woodbine, Georgia

(PICTURED ON PAGE 87)

PUDDING:
- 1/2 cup light molasses
- 1/2 cup hot water
- 2 teaspoons baking soda
- 1-1/2 cups all-purpose flour
- 2 cups fresh *or* frozen cranberries
- 1/2 teaspoon salt

SAUCE:
- 1 cup sugar
- 1 teaspoon cornstarch

Dash salt
- 1 cup heavy cream
- 1/2 cup butter *or* margarine
- 1 teaspoon vanilla extract

In a mixing bowl, combine all pudding ingredients in order given. Pour into a well-greased 4-cup pudding mold. Place in a deep kettle on a rack. Fill kettle with boiling water to 1-in. depth; cover kettle and boil gently. Replace water as needed. Steam about 1 hour or until pudding tests done. Let stand 5 minutes before removing from mold.

Meanwhile, prepare sauce by combining sugar, cornstarch and salt in a saucepan. Add cream and butter. Cook and stir over medium heat until mixture begins to boil. Boil for about 1 minute. Remove from the heat and stir in vanilla. Serve pudding and sauce warm. **Yield:** 6-8 servings.

FUDGE BROWNIES

Becky Albright, Norwalk, Ohio

(PICTURED ON PAGE 86)

- 1-1/3 cups all-purpose flour
- 2 cups sugar
- 3/4 cup baking cocoa
- 1 teaspoon baking powder
- 1/2 teaspoon salt
- 1/2 cup chopped nuts
- 2/3 cup cooking oil
- 4 eggs, slightly beaten
- 2 teaspoons vanilla extract

Combine flour, sugar, cocoa, baking powder, salt and nuts. Set aside. Combine oil, eggs and vanilla; add to dry ingredients. Do not overmix. Spread in a 13-in. x 9-in. x 2-in. baking pan. Bake at 350° for 20-25 minutes or until toothpick inserted in center comes out clean. **Yield:** about 2 dozen.

SOUR CREAM POUND CAKE

Karen Conrad, East Troy, Wisconsin

(PICTURED ON PAGE 87)

- 1 cup butter
- 3 cups sugar
- 6 eggs
- 1/4 teaspoon baking soda
- 2 teaspoons vanilla extract
- 1 cup (8 ounces) sour cream
- 3 cups all-purpose flour

Confectioners' sugar, optional

In a mixing bowl, cream butter and sugar. Add eggs, one at a time, beating well after each addition. Mix soda and vanilla with sour cream. Add alternately with the flour to the butter mixture. Mix well. Pour batter into a greased and floured tube pan. Bake at 325° for 80 minutes or until cake tests done. Cool in pan for 15 minutes before removing to a rack. Sprinkle with confectioners' sugar before serving, if desired. **Yield:** about 16 servings.

STRAWBERRY SHORTCAKE

Janet Becker, Anacortes, Washington

(PICTURED ON PAGE 87)

2/3 cup sugar
1/4 cup shortening
1 egg
1 teaspoon vanilla extract
1/4 teaspoon salt
1-1/2 cups all-purpose flour
2 teaspoons baking powder
1/2 cup milk
Whipped cream
1-1/2 quarts fresh *or* frozen strawberries, sliced

In a mixing bowl, cream sugar and shortening. Add egg and vanilla; beat well. Combine dry ingredients and add alternately with milk to the creamed mixture. Spread in a greased 9-in. x 9-in. baking pan. Bake at 350° for 20-25 minutes. Cool on wire rack. Cut into 9 servings. Split each serving horizontally and fill with whipped cream and strawberries. Replace top of cake; garnish with more berries and a dollop of whipped cream. Serve immediately. **Yield:** 9 servings.

STRAWBERRY CREAM PUFFS

Sherry Adams, Mt. Ayr, Iowa

(PICTURED ON PAGE 88)

1 cup water
1/2 cup butter *or* margarine
1 teaspoon sugar
1/4 teaspoon salt
1 cup all-purpose flour
4 eggs
CREAM FILLING:
2 pints fresh strawberries, sliced
1/2 cup sugar, *divided*
2 cups whipping cream
Confectioners' sugar
Additional sliced strawberries
Mint leaves

In a large saucepan, bring water, butter, sugar and salt to a boil. Add flour all at once and stir until a smooth ball forms. Remove from the heat and beat in eggs, one at a time. Continue beating until mixture is smooth and shiny.

Drop by tablespoonfuls 2 in. apart on a large ungreased cookie sheet (make 10). Bake at 400° for about 35 minutes or until golden brown. Cool on a wire rack. For filling, combine berries and 1/4 cup sugar. Chill 30 minutes. Beat cream and remaining sugar until stiff. Just before serving, cut tops off puffs. Combine berries and cream mixture. Fill cream puffs and replace tops. Sprinkle with confectioners' sugar, and garnish with additional berries and mint leaves. **Yield:** 10 cream puffs.

OLD-FASHIONED RICE CUSTARD

Shirley Leister, West Chester, Pennsylvania

(PICTURED ON PAGE 87)

1/2 cup uncooked long-grain rice
4 cups milk, *divided*
1/4 cup butter *or* margarine
3 eggs
3/4 cup sugar
1 teaspoon vanilla extract
1/4 teaspoon salt
1/2 teaspoon ground nutmeg

In the top of a double boiler, combine rice and 2 cups milk. Cook, stirring occasionally, over boiling water until rice is tender and most of the milk has evaporated, about 45 minutes. Stir in butter. Beat eggs; blend in sugar, vanilla, salt and remaining milk. Stir into the hot rice mixture. Pour into a lightly greased 2-qt. casserole and top with nutmeg. Bake at 350° for 50 minutes or until firm. **Yield:** 6-8 servings.

BUTTER PECAN ICE CREAM

Patricia Simms, Dallas, Texas

(PICTURED ON PAGE 88)

TOASTED NUTS:
3 tablespoons butter, melted
3/4 cup chopped pecans
1/8 teaspoon salt
1 tablespoon sugar
ICE CREAM:
1/2 cup packed brown sugar
1/4 cup sugar
2 tablespoons cornstarch
2 eggs, beaten
1/3 cup maple-flavored pancake syrup
2-1/2 cups milk
1 cup whipping cream
2 teaspoons vanilla extract

On a baking sheet, combine butter, pe-

cans, salt and 1 tablespoon sugar and spread into a single layer. Roast at 350° for 15 minutes. Stir and roast 15 minutes longer. Cool. For ice cream, combine sugars, cornstarch, eggs and syrup in the top of a double boiler. Gradually add milk. Cook over boiling water until mixture thickens. Remove from the heat and chill for several hours or overnight. Stir in nuts, cream and vanilla. Place in ice cream freezer and freeze according to manufacturer's directions. Allow to ripen in ice cream freezer or firm up in your refrigerator freezer an hour before serving. **Yield:** about 2 quarts.

GRANDMA'S CHOCOLATE MERINGUE PIE

Donna Vest Tilley, Chesterfield, Virginia

(PICTURED ON PAGE 88)

3/4 cup sugar
5 tablespoons baking cocoa
3 tablespoons cornstarch
1/4 teaspoon salt
2 cups milk
3 egg yolks, beaten
1 teaspoon vanilla extract
1 pie shell (9 inches), baked
MERINGUE:
3 egg whites
1/4 teaspoon cream of tartar
6 tablespoons sugar

In a saucepan, mix sugar, cocoa, cornstarch and salt; gradually add milk. Cook and stir over medium-high heat until thickened and bubbly. Reduce heat; cook and stir 2 minutes more. Remove from heat. Stir about 1 cup of the hot filling into the egg yolks. Return to saucepan and bring to a gentle boil. Cook and stir 2 minutes. Remove from the heat and stir in vanilla. Pour *hot* filling into pie crust. For meringue, immediately beat egg whites with cream of tartar until soft peaks form. Gradually add sugar and continue to beat until stiff and glossy. Spread evenly over hot filling, sealing meringue to pie crust. Bake at 350° for 12-15 minutes or until golden. **Yield:** 8 servings.

NOT-TOO-HOT CHOCOLATE: Chocolate scorches easily, so melt it slowly over hot water. Don't let the water boil—the steam may harden or stiffen the chocolate. If this happens, reliquify it by stirring in 1/2 teaspoon vegetable shortening (not butter) for each ounce of chocolate.

MEMORABLE MEAL

The following four recipes come from Lydia Robotewskyj of Franklin, Wisconsin (see photo and story on page 90).

◆◆◆

SPICED APPLE PORK ROAST

1 rolled boneless pork loin roast (4 to 5 pounds)
1 garlic clove, cut into lengthwise strips
2 tablespoons all-purpose flour
1 teaspoon salt
1/2 teaspoon sugar
1 teaspoon prepared mustard
1/8 teaspoon pepper
1 cup applesauce
1/3 cup packed brown sugar
2 teaspoons vinegar
1/8 to 1/4 teaspoon ground cloves

Remove and discard all excess fat from roast. Cut slits in top of roast; insert garlic strips. Mix the flour with salt, sugar, mustard and pepper. Rub over the roast. Place the meat, fat side up, on a rack in a roasting pan. Bake at 325° for 30-40 minutes *per pound* or until the internal temperature reaches 160°-170°. Combine applesauce, brown sugar, vinegar and cloves; generously brush over roast during last half hour of baking. **Yield:** 12-15 servings.

◆◆◆

COUNTRY POTATO PANCAKES

3 large potatoes (about 2 pounds), peeled
2 eggs, slightly beaten
1 tablespoon grated onion
2 tablespoons all-purpose flour
1 teaspoon salt
1/2 teaspoon baking powder

Vegetable oil

Finely grate potatoes. Drain any liquid. Add eggs, onion, flour, salt and baking powder. In a frying pan, add oil to the depth of 1/8 in.; heat over medium-high (375°). Drop batter by heaping tablespoonfuls in hot oil. Flatten to form patties. Fry until golden brown then turn and cook other side. Serve immediately. **Yield:** about 24 pancakes.

◆◆◆

SOUR CREAM CUCUMBER SALAD

✓ This tasty dish uses less sugar, salt and fat. Recipe includes *Diabetic Exchanges*.

3 medium cucumbers, peeled and thinly sliced
1/2 teaspoon salt
1/2 cup finely chopped green onions
1 tablespoon white vinegar
Dash white pepper
1/4 cup sour cream

Sprinkle the cucumbers with salt. Let stand 15 minutes. Drain liquid. Add onions, vinegar and pepper. Just before serving, stir in sour cream. **Yield:** 6 servings. **Diabetic Exchanges:** One serving (prepared with light sour cream) equals 1 vegetable; also, 35 calories, 197 mg sodium, 2 mg cholesterol, 6 gm carbohydrate, 2 gm protein, 1 gm fat.

◆◆◆

BABKA (NOODLE PUDDING)

1 pound egg noodles *or* spaghetti
1/2 cup butter *or* margarine, melted
10 eggs
3/4 cup milk
1 cup sugar
Cherry, apricot *or* strawberry preserves

Cook noodles in boiling salted water until almost done. Drain. Place in a mixing bowl with butter; toss to coat. In a separate bowl, beat eggs, milk and sugar until well blended. Combine with noodles. Pour into a greased 13-in. x 9-in. x 2-in. baking dish. Bake at 350° for about 35 minutes or until puffy and noodles begin to brown at edges. Cut into squares and serve hot or cold with fruit preserves. **Yield:** 12 servings.

◆◆◆

FAMILY CHEESECAKE SQUARES

Loretta Ruda, Kennesaw, Georgia

(PICTURED ON PAGE 88)

CRUST:
1 package (1/4 ounce) active dry yeast
1/4 cup warm milk (105°-110°)
1 tablespoon sugar
1 cup butter *or* margarine
2-1/2 cups all-purpose flour
1/2 teaspoon salt
4 egg yolks, slightly beaten
FILLING:
1 egg, *separated*
2 packages (8 ounces *each*) cream cheese, softened
1 cup sugar
1 teaspoon vanilla extract
1/2 cup chopped pecans

Dissolve yeast in warm milk; add sugar and set aside. In a large mixing bowl, cut butter into flour and salt as for pie crust. Add yolks and yeast mixture. Mix thoroughly. Divide dough into two parts. Roll each piece to fit a 13-in. x 9-in. x 2-in. baking pan. Place one piece in pan. For filling, beat yolk, cream cheese, sugar and vanilla until smooth. Spread over dough and cover with remaining dough. Press lightly to seal edges around pan. Brush top with slightly beaten egg white and sprinkle with nuts. Cover and allow to rise in a warm place 1-1/2 hours. Bake at 350° for 30-35 minutes or until lightly browned. Cut into squares to serve. **Yield:** 24 servings.

◆◆◆

SAUSAGE-STUFFED MUSHROOMS

Beatrice Vetrano, Landenberg, Pennsylvania

12 to 15 large fresh mushrooms
2 tablespoons butter *or* margarine, *divided*
2 tablespoons chopped onion
1 tablespoon lemon juice
1/4 teaspoon dried basil
Salt and pepper to taste
4 ounces bulk Italian sausage
1 tablespoon chopped fresh parsley
2 tablespoons dried bread crumbs
2 tablespoons grated Parmesan cheese

Remove stems from the mushrooms. Chop stems finely; reserve caps. Place stems in paper towel and squeeze to remove any liquid. In a skillet, heat 1-

1/2 tablespoons butter. Cook stems and onion until soft. Add lemon juice, basil, salt and pepper; cook until almost all the liquid has evaporated. Cool. Combine mushroom mixture with sausage and parsley. Stuff into the mushroom caps. Combine crumbs and cheese; sprinkle over stuffed mushrooms. Dot each with remaining butter. Place in a greased baking pan and bake at 400° for 20 minutes. Baste occasionally with pan juices. Serve hot. **Yield:** 12-15 servings.

CRANBERRY MEATBALLS

Helen Wiegmink, Tucson, Arizona

- 1 pound lean ground beef
- 1 egg, slightly beaten
- 1/2 cup crushed saltine crackers
- 1/2 small onion, diced
- 1 teaspoon salt
- 1/2 teaspoon pepper
- 1 can (16 ounces) whole cranberry sauce
- 1 can (10-3/4 ounces) cream of tomato soup, undiluted

Cooked rice *or* noodles

In a mixing bowl, combine first six ingredients. Shape into 1-1/2-in. balls. Place on a rack in a baking pan. Bake at 400° for 20 minutes. Meanwhile, combine cranberry sauce and tomato soup. Heat through. Add meatballs and simmer 10 minutes. Serve with rice or noodles. May also be used as an appetizer. **Yield:** 4 main-dish servings. **If Cooking for Two:** Freeze half the cooked meatballs for another meal.

RED RIVER BEEF STROGANOFF

Mary Alice Cox, Clinton, Tennessee

- 2 pounds sirloin steak, cut into thin strips
- 1/4 cup all-purpose flour
- 1/2 cup butter *or* margarine, *divided*
- 2 large onions, chopped
- 1 can (10-1/2 ounces) beef broth
- 1 teaspoon dried basil

Salt and pepper to taste

- 1 jar (4-1/2 ounces) sliced mushrooms, drained
- 1 tablespoon Worcestershire sauce
- 1 cup (8 ounces) sour cream

Cooked rice *or* noodles

Dredge meat in flour. In a skillet, melt 1/4 cup butter over medium heat; saute onions until tender. Remove from pan; set aside. Melt remaining butter and brown meat on all sides. Add broth, basil, salt and pepper, mushrooms, Worcestershire sauce and onions. Cook until mixture thickens, about 5 minutes. Just before serving, stir in sour cream. Heat through, but do not boil. Serve immediately over rice or noodles. **Yield:** 8 servings.

CHEESY ONION CASSEROLE

Beth Perry, Jacksonville, Florida

- 2 tablespoons butter *or* margarine
- 3 large sweet white onions, sliced
- 2 cups (8 ounces) shredded Swiss cheese, *divided*

Pepper to taste

- 1 can (10-3/4 ounces) cream of chicken soup, undiluted
- 2/3 cup milk
- 1 teaspoon soy sauce
- 8 slices French bread, buttered on both sides

In a skillet, melt butter. Saute onions until clear and slightly brown. Layer onions, two-thirds of the cheese and the pepper in a 2-qt. casserole. In a saucepan, heat soup, milk and soy sauce; stir to blend. Pour soup mixture into casserole and stir gently. Top with bread slices. Bake at 350° for 15 minutes. Push bread slices down under sauce; sprinkle with remaining cheese. Bake 15 minutes more. This is good served as a side dish with beef or pork roast. **Yield:** 8 servings.

AFTER-THE-HOLIDAYS SALAD

Gladys Kirsch, Mott, North Dakota

- 2 cups diced cooked turkey
- 1 cup pineapple chunks, well drained
- 1 cup diced celery
- 1/2 cup sliced green onions
- 1/4 cup dry roasted peanuts
- 1 cup seedless green grapes
- 2/3 cup mayonnaise
- 2 tablespoons chopped chutney
- 1 tablespoon lime juice
- 1/2 teaspoon curry powder
- 1/4 teaspoon salt

Lettuce leaves, optional

In a mixing bowl, toss first six ingredients. In a small bowl, combine all remaining ingredients except lettuce. Pour over turkey mixture and mix gently. Chill. Serve on a bed of lettuce, if desired. **Yield:** 4 servings.

POPCORN CARAMEL CRUNCH

Lucille Hermsmeyer, Scotia, Nebraska

- 4 cups popped popcorn
- 1 cup dry roasted peanuts
- 1 cup chow mein noodles
- 1/2 cup raisins
- 1 cup sugar
- 3/4 cup butter
- 1/2 cup light corn syrup
- 2 tablespoons water
- 1 teaspoon ground cinnamon

In a large greased bowl, combine first four ingredients. Set aside. In a large saucepan, combine sugar, butter, corn syrup and water. Cook over medium heat, stirring occasionally, until mixture reaches soft crack stage (280°-290°) with a candy thermometer. Remove from the heat. Stir in cinnamon. Pour over popcorn mixture; stir until all ingredients are evenly coated. Immediately pour onto a greased 15-in. x 10-in. x 1-in. pan. When cool enough to handle, break into pieces. Store in covered containers to enjoy later or to give as gifts. **Yield:** about 8 cups.

BUTTERHORNS

Bernice Smith, Sturgeon Lake, Minnesota

- 4 cups all-purpose flour
- 1/2 cup sugar
- 1 teaspoon salt
- 1 cup butter, margarine *or* shortening
- 1 package (1/4 ounce) active dry yeast
- 1/4 cup warm water (110°-115°)
- 3/4 cup warm milk (110°-115°)
- 1 egg, lightly beaten
- 1/4 cup butter *or* margarine, melted, *divided*

In a large bowl, combine flour, sugar and salt. Cut in butter as for pie crust; set aside. Dissolve yeast in water. Add with the milk and egg to the flour mixture; mix well. Cover and refrigerate overnight. The next day, divide dough into four equal parts. On a lightly floured board, roll each portion into a 12-in. circle. Brush with 1 tablespoon melted butter and cut into 12 pie-shaped wedges. Roll up, beginning with the wide end, and place on greased cookie sheets. Repeat with remaining dough. Cover and let rise in a warm place until nearly doubled, about 1 hour. Bake at 375° for 10-12 minutes or until golden brown. **Yield:** 48 rolls. **If Cooking for Two:** Freeze butterhorns in a plastic bag. Defrost as needed.

F

Fruit *(also see specific kinds)*
Cantaloupe and Raspberry Melba, 54
Fruit Pizza, 48
Layered Fresh Fruit Salad, 60
Melon Balls with Lime Sauce, 66
Winter Fruit Salad, 17

G

Ground Beef
Beef/Mushroom Pockets, 64
Beef-Stuffed Squash, 16
Chili Skillet, 12
Cranberry Meatballs, 94
Donna's Lasagna, 9
German Meatballs, 30
German Pizza, 12
Hoosier Chili, 79
Lasagna Rolls, 34
Meatball Garden Stew, 13
Meatball Minestrone, 62
Peoria Chili, 14
Picadillo in Pita Bread, 11
Poor Man's Filet Mignon, 48
Pronto Chili, 7
Ranch-Style Baked Lentils, 17
Shipwreck Stew, 15
Skillet Lasagna, 16
Summer Stuffed Peppers, 48

H

Ham
Best-Ever Asparagus/Ham Rolls, 44
Grandma's Pea Soup, 16
Ham and Asparagus Au Gratin, 45
Hearty Ham Loaf, 31
Swiss and Ham Pie, 70
White Lasagna, 80

I

Ice Cream
Butter Pecan Ice Cream, 93
Lemon/Orange Ice, 61
Milky Way Ice Cream, 30

L

Lamb
Braised Lamb Shanks, 53
Lasagna
Donna's Lasagna, 9
Lasagna Rolls, 34
Skillet Lasagna, 16
White Lasagna, 80
Lemon
California Lemon Pound Cake, 28
Citrus-Baked Cornish Hens, 61
Golden Lemon Glazed Cheesecake, 60
Lemon Butter Topping, 66
Lemon Custard in Meringue Cups, 62
Lemon/Orange Ice, 61
Luscious Lemon Pie, 31
Mexican Carnitas, 61
Orange Lemonade, 61
Tangy Citrus Dressing, 66

Zesty Lemon Curd, 60

M

Meals in Minutes
❖ Pronto Chili/Corn Bread/Banana Cream Parfait, 7
❖ Lasagna Rolls/Dilled Vegetable Salad/Angel Food Torte, 34
❖ Minute Steaks Parmesan/Italian Salad Bowl/Honey Buttered Corn/Peach Melba Dessert, 39
❖ Chicken and Potato Saute/Garden Medley/Cantaloupe and Raspberry Melba, 54
❖ Quick Vegetable Soup/Toasty Garlic Bread/Caramel Dumplings, 69
Memorable Meals
❖ Peoria Chili/Mom's Corn Bread/Devil's Food Cake/Hot Cinnamon Cocoa, 14
❖ Hearty Ham Loaf/Cauliflower Au Gratin/Golden Dinner Rolls/Strawberry Glaze Pie, 31
❖ Meatball Minestrone/Baked Rigatoni/Marinated Vegetables/Anise Cookies, 62
❖ Spiced Apple Pork Roast/Country Potato Pancakes/Sour Cream Cucumber Salad/Babka (Noodle Pudding), 94
Muffins
Apricot Muffins, 48
Cornmeal Muffins, 81
Cranberry Muffins, 27
Orange Blueberry Muffins, 63
Orange Cream Cheese Muffins, 44
Orange Tea Muffins, 61
Whole Wheat English Muffins, 81
Mushroom
Beef/Mushroom Pockets, 64
Chicken Mushroom Stir-Fry, 13
Marinated Mushrooms, 48
Sausage-Stuffed Mushrooms, 95
Turkey Mushroom Supreme, 81

N

Nuts
Almond Asparagus, 43
Breakfast Granola, 21
Butter Pecan Ice Cream, 93
Date Nut Torte, 92
Mandarin Almond Salad, 49
Never-Fail Pecan Pie, 15
Pineapple Pecan Cheese Ball, 28
Popcorn Caramel Crunch, 95

O

Onion
Cheesy Onion Casserole, 95
Dad's Onion Rings, 65
Orange and Red Onion Salad, 61
Orange
Citrus-Baked Cornish Hens, 61
Double Orange Cookies, 50
Lemon/Orange Ice, 61
Mandarin Almond Salad, 49
Mexican Carnitas, 61
Orange and Red Onion Salad, 61
Orange Barbecued Turkey, 66

Orange Beef and Broccoli Stir-Fry, 17
Orange Blueberry Muffins, 63
Orange Colada, 66
Orange Cream Cheese Muffins, 44
Orange Lemonade, 61
Orange Pork Chops, 60
Orange Tea Muffins, 61
Spicy Citrus Salad, 79
Sunshine Chicken, 80
Tangy Citrus Dressing, 66

P

Pancakes
Apple Pancake, 85
Brown Sugar Oatmeal Pancakes, 63
Country Potato Pancakes, 94
Kaiserschmarren, 85
Pasta
Baked Rigatoni, 62
Herbed Macaroni and Cheese, 15
Pasta with Asparagus, 46
Shrimp and Pasta Supper, 63
Peach
Blueberry and Peach Cobbler, 89
Freeze-Ahead Peach Pie Filling, 89
Fresh Peach Crisp, 21
Peach Melba Dessert, 39
Peppers
Garden Medley, 54
Southwestern Beef Brisket, 75
Spicy Beef with Peppers, 12
Summer Stuffed Peppers, 48
Pies
Candy Bar Pie, 22
Cherry Berry Pie, 59
Chocolate Malt Shoppe Pie, 29
Freeze-Ahead Peach Pie Filling, 89
Grammy Gilman's Raisin Pie, 89
Grandma's Chocolate Meringue Pie, 93
Luscious Lemon Pie, 31
Never-Fail Pecan Pie, 15
Peanut Butter Pie, 9
Perfect Apple Pie, 21
Raspberry/Lime Pie, 66
Strawberry Glaze Pie, 31
Sweet Potato Pie, 75
Upstate Chocolate Peanut Butter Pie, 16
Pizza
Chocolate Pizza, 22
Fruit Pizza, 48
German Pizza, 12
Skillet Pizza, 11
Pork
Fruited Chops, 12
Mexican Carnitas, 61
Orange Pork Chops, 60
Pork Oriental, 9
Roast Pork Loin, 18
Speidis, 59
Spiced Apple Pork Roast, 94
Sweet and Sour Pork, 11
Zesty Grilled Chops, 44
Potatoes
Chicken and Potato Saute, 54
Country Potato Pancakes, 94
Crisp Hash for Two, 31
German Pizza, 12
Grandma's Potato Salad, 27
Greek Roasted Chicken and Potatoes, 78
Mashed Potato Doughnuts, 70
Parmesan Potato Rounds, 59
Potato Soup with Sausage, 65
Wisconsin Potato Cheese Soup, 75
Pudding
Babka (Noodle Pudding), 94